SORTING IT OUT

SORTING IT OUT

DISCERNING GOD'S CALL TO MINISTRY

ALICE R. CULLINAN

Judson Press

Valley Forge

Library of Congress Cataloging-in-Publication Data
Cullinan, Alice R.
    Sorting it out: discerning God's call to ministry / Alice R. Cullinan.
        p. cm.
    Includes bibliographical references
    ISBN 0-8170-1302-4 (pbk. : alk. paper)
        1. Clergy – Appointment, call, and election. 2. Clergy – Office. I. Title.
    BV4011.4.C85 1999
    253'.2 – dc21   98-49515

Printed in the U.S.A.
06 05 04
10 9 8 7 6 5 4

Dedicated with thanksgiving to our wonderful Lord,
who continues to call men and women to Christian ministry,
and to all those who are seeking to understand
this call for their own lives.

CONTENTS

INTRODUCTION

The church leaders found it important to plan a missionary emphasis in the fall of each year, and this year was no exception. The speaker was a woman serving as a missionary in Japan. During her presentation, a young college freshman felt a strange tug at her heart. Although she did not go forward in response to the invitation, she did speak to the pastor at the close of the service.

"I think God may be calling me into some kind of ministry," she told him, "but how can I know for sure?"

"Come by the office this week, and we'll talk about it," he answered. "I don't have any magical answers, but I'll be happy to share with you some things that may be of help."

A few days later the two met for a conference. The young student had been a Christian for only a year, but she felt comfortable talking with her pastor. He had baptized her and had been available and helpful in answering the many questions she had about her new life as a Christian.

"Let me start by sharing with you about my own call into ministry," he said. "Then we will look at some principles that have helped others, as well as some Scriptures that may help. And I want you to remember that you must not expect the Lord to give you the whole blueprint of your life all at once."

Several weeks passed after their discussion. One Sunday morning during the invitation portion of the service, the young woman made her way to the front of the sanctuary to share her commitment with the pastor and the congregation. She was now convinced that what she experienced in the service when the missionary was speaking was God's call to ministry. Her pastor reminded her that she did not need to know the specifics. "Just faithfully walk with the Lord," he said, "and he will let you know all the information when you need to know it."

Many years passed, and the young woman continued to follow God's leadership. She completed her studies at college and seminary and was invited to serve as minister of music and education on a church staff in Virginia. She later earned a Ph.D. and served on staff at the Virginia Baptist State Convention, teaching others how to teach Sunday school more effectively.

The next step in God's plan was an invitation to be a professor of Religion and Religious Education at a Baptist university in North Carolina. I have served for over twenty years as a university professor. Little did I know what God had in store for me when I answered the call to vocational Christian ministry. I am joyfully investing my life helping others follow God's call for their lives.

Much of what I share with you in this book I have learned from personal experience and in conversations with others. Some I have learned from research conducted while on a sabbatical leave from the university. I am indebted to the 365 men and women who responded to a survey I conducted of those who have felt and answered God's call to ministry.

My heartfelt prayer is that God might speak to you through this book if you are struggling to discern a call to ministry or vocational placement within the call. For those of you who are faithfully serving the Lord in some vocational ministry, I hope the book will inspire you to continue doing so, even when difficulties arise and discouragement abounds. Perhaps you will glean some specific information that will help you counsel others who ask for help in these areas.

For those of you who are God's lay ministers, I pray that the information I share with you about hearing God's voice, using your gifts, and following God's will for you will be especially helpful, even if you discover the Lord wants you to serve in a ministry that is not vocational (i.e., full-time). And I hope that some who read the book will be challenged to hear God's call to bivocational ministry, an area often overlooked but much needed in God's harvest field.

Chapter One

DEFINING A CALL
TO MINISTRY

A divinity school student stayed after class one day to share with me how God had called him out of a law practice into the preaching ministry. "I was good at what I did, and found satisfaction in it. But I just could not get away from that tug at my heart that I am supposed to be a preacher. I am in my first church now, and I cannot tell you the joy I feel from being in the center of God's will for my life!"

Another student came by my office to tell me he had read the materials I had put together on the call to ministry. "Dr. C., I believe I am going to change my major to business. I have peace now that God wants me to serve in the business world, not in ministry as I had first thought. I now know that God was interested in the commitment of my life *to* him, not in just doing a job *for* him."

I received a letter from a former student who was in his first year of seminary. He was an older student who had served in the armed services before following what he perceived as a call.

"I know you may have wondered what happened to me," he wrote. "I guess you remember how many questions I had when I was a student at [Gardner-Webb University]. I just couldn't seem to get clear direction about my call. . . . I believe the Lord wants me to be a bi-vocational minister, to earn my livelihood in what some call a secular field, while serving God in a small church. I can't tell you how happy I am finally to know that this kind of ministry is not second rate, and that God had this planned for me all along. I just was unwilling to see it."

1

One difficulty we face when trying to discover whether God has called us to ministry is understanding the questions and terms involved. What is ministry? What is a call? Aren't all Christians called to minister? Does the call come only to those who enter vocational ministry? What exactly *is* vocational ministry? Is the call to ministry always a call to the pastorate? Does the call to ministry always mean serving on a church staff? Is a call to preach different from a call to other vocational ministries? Is a call to the mission field different from the initial call to vocational ministry? Are there calls that are different from vocational calls? What about bi-vocational ministry? Does a call from God ever change?

We will discuss some of these issues in this chapter. Others will become clearer as we proceed through the book. Still others will take a lifetime of walking with God to understand. But we must make a start in answering these questions before we continue.

"Vocation" comes from the Latin word *vocare,* meaning "to call or summons." It implies someone who does the calling and someone to whom the call is addressed. In the case of vocational ministry, God is the "someone" who calls, and we, God's children, are the ones to whom the call is addressed.

The biblical word for vocation or calling is the Greek *kaleō.* Paul used the word in writing to the church at Ephesus: "As a prisoner for the Lord, then, I urge you to live a life worthy of the *calling* [vocation in KJV] you have received" (Ephesians 4:1 NIV).

According to Henlee Barnette, in his book *Has God Called You?,* the term and its derivatives are used almost two hundred times in the Gospels and Epistles. They only have theological meaning, however, seventy times, forty of which are in Paul's writings.[1] Each of these times the word refers solely to the call of God to salvation, which includes service. Felix Montgomery agrees, observing that this "calling was not to an occupation but to a relationship of faith in God and obedience to his purpose."[2]

Although much of the emphasis on the word translated "calling" in the New Testament refers to the general calling of all Christians to respond to the gospel, some contexts involve the concept of calling individuals to specific ministries and places of ministry, as in the Scriptures cited below.

> Set apart for me Barnabas and Saul for the work to which I have called them. (Acts 13:2)

> During the night Paul had a vision of a man of Macedonia standing and begging him, "Come over to Macedonia and help us." After Paul had seen the vision, we got ready at once to leave for Macedonia, concluding that God had called us to preach the gospel to them. (Acts 16:9–10)

The biblical word for ministry is *diakonia,* translated "service." From another form of the word, *diakonos* or "servant," we derive our word "deacon." The Greek terms encompass both service in a general, domestic sense as well as service in a spiritual and religious sense. Like the biblical understanding of calling, biblical reference to ministry involves the responsibility and work of all believers *and* the particular apostolic ministry of specific persons. The ambiguity exists in English as well. As a result, some people have suggested that we use the word "ministers" with a lower case "m" to describe all Christians and use "Ministers" with an upper case "M" to designate those whose service is set apart for the sake of the church in its mission to the world. The justification for such a distinction, these people say, is based on Romans 12:6–8, 1 Corinthians 12:4–11, and Ephesians 4:4–16.

The term *ecclesia,* translated "church," means literally "called-out ones," implying a corporate call to be involved in God's work of redemption for the world. As Barnette observes, "Every person who responds to God's call is a minister, a member of the priesthood of all believers, with priestly functions."[3] However, Ephesians 4 suggests that some believers are gifted for the sake of the entire body, to help others develop their spiritual gifts needed to answer the corporate call to minister to the world.

The debate surrounding the issue continues. Is the call to ministry for all Christians or for only some? In a general sense, isn't ministry to be a way of life for all Christians? On the other hand, don't some individuals receive a call to enter a specific vocation beyond the life of service expected of all Christians — namely, a professional ministry?

Barnette insists that "all Christians are called to be ministers regardless of their occupations in life."[4] He believes that God's call must never be considered exclusively vocational in nature. The call to ministry, he says, must embrace the Christian's entire life. Some will continue in their jobs, as did Paul. Others will depend upon the church for their living, as did Peter. Regardless of the means of self-support, a Christian is to minister, answering the call of God to "full-life service."

As I worked on the manuscript for this book, I e-mailed surveys to people over the Internet. My note, posted on appropriate bulletin boards, solicited responses from anyone who had experienced a call to ministry. One of the respondents raised a question regarding the term "ministry."

> I, too, once believed that I was called to the pastorate. Perhaps someday I will try this occupation. However, I presently have a more urgent calling: serve God where he places me, today, now, here, by being a witness to the one or two hurting people he brings into my life. I minister where I am, when I can. I just wish pastors and churches would celebrate such unofficial ministers a little more often.

Like Barnette, this Internet respondent was concerned that we abolish the distinction between sacred and secular callings. Barnette, however, acknowledged that within the general call to all Christians, there are particular callings to various ministries, determined by the spiritual gifts one possesses. "But this does not make them superior to the church or to their fellow Christians," he writes.[5]

Others who have written on the subject of the call agree with Barnette. In his book *God Calls Me*, J. Winston Pearce writes, "Every Christian should be called of God to the work in which he is engaged, not just the person engaged in some church-related task."[6] Franklin Segler, author of *A Theology of Church and Ministry*, states, "It is not valid to consider the gospel ministry as the only vocation into which men are called by God to serve their generation." He did mention, however, that Christian ministry is a "unique call," and he used the Bible and church history to support this opinion.[7]

More recently, Dennis M. Campbell states in his book, *Who Will Go for Us?,* "Christian vocation refers not to a certain group of jobs, such as the pastorate, or other full-time positions of leadership in the church, but to all of the varied roles Christians play in the world."[8]

Certainly God calls each of us to minister to others in Christ's name. But what does the Bible mean when it says that individuals have had a special call from God to undertake a particular task or mission? What about thousands of people through the ages who have testified to a "special" call, one that seems to go beyond the call that others hear? What about Peter Marshall, Billy Graham, Charles Wesley, Charles Spurgeon, and hundreds of other well-known ministers who have testified of God's special call on their lives? What about your own pastor and staff members and thousands of others like them? What about the missionaries whose testimonies you have heard, and the college or seminary professors who labor under the call of God on their lives? Ask the hundreds of students who are in school now preparing for ministry, having answered a "special call" to commit their lives to vocational ministry.

Theologian H. Richard Niebuhr identified the following four elements as essential characteristics of a call to ministry: (1) *the call to be a Christian,* meaning to become a disciple of Jesus; (2) *the secret call,* defined as the experience of feeling "summoned or invited by God to take up the work of the ministry"; (3) *the providential call,* which is apparent when an individual's aptitudes, abilities, circumstances, and inner spiritual drive match the need; and (4) *the ecclesiastical call,* which comes from a specific church or institution, inviting an individual to serve there.[9]

The *call to be a disciple* of Jesus is obviously the most important calling in life. When we answer that call to salvation and discipleship, we must obediently serve and minister to others in the name of Jesus. But what about the *secret call?* Is there a call to individual Christians to serve a "special" way, in some form of vocational ministry that differs from the vocation of being a nurse, lawyer, or counselor?

According to John Calvin, yes, there is a secret call, "of which every minister is conscious."[10] Oswald Chambers adds some thoughts to this discussion:

> The realization of the call in a person's life may come like a clap of thunder or it may dawn gradually. But however quickly or slowly this awareness comes, it is always accompanied with an undercurrent of the supernatural — something that is inexpressible and produces a "glow." At any moment the sudden awareness of this incalculable, supernatural, surprising call that has taken hold of your life may break through — "I chose you."[11]

The assumption upon which this book is written is that while all Christians are called to minister in their roles as disciples of Christ, for some there is a secret call to minister in specific ways in God's kingdom. Those who have experienced such a "secret call" know its validity. Multitudes have experienced what they describe as a unique call to ministry, one that goes beyond their call to discipleship. Their experiences are as varied as the individuals themselves.

History of the Call

Evidence of the special call of God to human beings has been around for centuries. "The oldest profession in all of history is the religious profession. Indeed interesting documentation for the religious calling as profession can be found as far back as the numerous tablets from Mesopotamia, c. 2000–1800 B.C."[12]

The divine call to God's people is a recurring theme in the Bible. "Where are you?" comes the call when we disobey and are out of fellowship with God. "You will be my people and I will be your God" is the call to relationship and fellowship. "You shall have no other gods before me" is a call to commitment. "I have given you as a covenant to the people" is a call to service.

Some scholars believe, however, that in the early church, there was no obvious difference between the clergy (*kleros*) and the laity (*laos*); accepting Jesus as Lord meant ministering to others in his name. Other people assert that the early church *did* have a clear understanding of differing roles of leadership and "calling." Paul spoke often of having been "made an apostle." He gave explicit instructions regarding the qualifications of elders and deacons, and he consulted the apostles in Jerusalem whenever the question of Gentile Christians became an issue.

Clement of Rome (c. 95) was completely convinced that the Lord had established a "due order."

> [B]y his own supreme will, he himself appointed the place and ministers of their performance, that all might be done according to his good pleasure and so be acceptable to his will. . . . To the high priest are given his special ministrations, a special place is reserved for the priests, and special duties are imposed upon the Levites, while the layman is bound by the ordinances concerning the laity.[13]

According to Glenn Hinson, Clement was the first Christian writer to use the term "laity," and he spoke of laity as belonging to an *ordo,* just as the clergy did. In the minds of some, Hinson writes, their baptism was their ordination as layperson.[14]

The earliest use of clergy (*kleros*) was by Tertullian, about A.D. 208. In his writings entitled, *De praescriptione haereticorum,* he wrote that "if Jesus Christ sent out the Apostles to preach, no others are to be accepted as preachers but those whom Christ appointed." He went on to say, however, "Are not we laymen priests, also?"[15]

The real division in the concepts of laity versus clergy seemed to develop in the fourth century when Christianity was established as the state religion, at which time the role of clergy was transformed into a civil service with political and economic status. The chasm between clergy and laity widened during the Middle Ages.[16]

During the Reformation the idea of two paths in life changed. The priestly life for those called to perfection and the ordinary path for those whose duty lay in the secular world was replaced with the idea that all Christians are called into a life of service and holiness, in whatever occupation they strive. There remained, however, an emphasis on a "call." In the section on

"Orders," the Confession of Augsburg, 1530, stated "no one ought to teach publicly in churches or to administer the sacraments, unless duly called."[17] *The Chief Principles of the Christian Religion, as professed by the people called the Quakers,* written in 1678, stated:

> [B]y the leading, moving and drawing hereof ought every Evangelist and Christian pastor to be led and ordered in his labour and work of the Gospel, both as to the place where, as to the persons to whom, and as to the times when, he is to minister.[18]

The lines between clergy and laity remain unclear, however. Some Christians still believe that the call to be a preacher or missionary is not any different from the call to be a farmer or teacher. Others testify to a "unique call" that is different from the layperson's "call" into a secular vocation. Perhaps the church itself has created some of the difficulties. As the respondent to my e-mail request remarked: "I just wish pastors and churches would celebrate such unofficial ministers a little more often."

Richard Broholm seems to agree in emphasizing the importance of the role of both clergy and laity:

> If we are not prepared to suggest that the calling of the religiously professional is a higher calling worthy of special recognition and confirmation, then we must either be prepared to do away with the ordination of clergy or move to provide for the ordination of lay persons to their ministry of service in the world. It seems to me the time has come, if we are serious about the validity of the ministry of laity, to recognize their special gifts and calling and to affirm and establish their ministry in the world with the same sense of care and significance that we attach to the calling of other members of the body. Lay persons need to be examined for the legitimacy of their call and the clarity about their gifts with the same kind of intentionality which today we focus on candidates for ordination. The traditional roles of clergy and laymen must be reversed: the laymen become the troops in the front line and the clergy, with the gathered church, help to support them. Until this revolution occurs, the Protestant concept of priesthood of all believers remains vague and unrealized.[19]

Those of us who, like me, affirm the uniqueness of a "special call" to ministry certainly support the need to recognize the laity for their gifts and needed ministries, but we cannot overlook the experiences of many Christians who witness to a calling that goes beyond their call to discipleship. Perhaps if we understand better the calls that God issues to each of us, we will gain some clarity in discerning whether or not we have experienced a "secret call."

Universal Calls

"Hey, Dr. C." Laura said as she stepped into my office one afternoon. "Got a minute?" she asked. "I need to bounce something off of you."

"Sure. Come on in," I replied. "I always try to make time for folks who are bouncing something friendly off my head!"

"You know how serious I am about wanting to do God's will for my life, Dr. C. I'm just having a hard time right now figuring out what that is. Can you help?"

Laura's question about understanding God's will is one I hear often from my students and one I ask quite often myself! How to determine the unique call of God for each of us as individuals is an important issue. Equally important is the recognition that certain calls come to every Christian. Coming to an understanding of these *universal* calls may be the best place to begin. Obedience in these areas may be the key to unlock information we need about God's *specific* will for us, especially as it relates to the call to ministry.

1. The call to salvation. Before you can respond to the call to ministry, you must first respond to the call of God for salvation. "Jesus answered, 'I have not come to call the righteous to salvation, but sinners'" (Matthew 9:13).

John was pastor of a small church while he was a student at seminary. During a revival at his church, an evangelist preached on being sure you have actually met the Lord. He explained how easy it is to accept a set of beliefs without knowing God personally. John's heart was strangely convicted by the Holy Spirit. After the service, he met with the evangelist to pray. During that time of prayer and conversation, John realized he had never invited the Lord into his heart to be his Savior.

> It is possible for a man to go through with all preparatory theological studies, to be ordained, and to officiate for years as a preacher of the gospel, when he has never felt its converting power in his own soul.[20]

2. The call to holiness. God also calls you to live a holy life, one that is set apart for the Lord's use. Scripture reminds us, "God did not call us to be impure, but to a holy life" (1 Thessalonians 4:7); "God has saved us and called us to a holy life" (2 Timothy 1:9).

I have been privileged for more than twenty years to work with hundreds of students who have come to our university to study for the ministry. I have noticed an increase in recent years in the numbers of students who have enrolled in our school, having spent many years in another vocation. Some of these older students have related to me how much they hate to study and prepare sermons, but they "feel God calling them to preach." As they grow in their spiritual walks with God, however, some have come to understand that their calling is not to the pastorate but to holiness. (Curiously, I have *not* noticed this same tendency in younger students.)

3. The call to praise. God expects your praise. "You are a chosen people, a royal priesthood, a holy nation, a people belonging to God, that you may declare the praises of him who called you out of darkness into his wonderful light" (1 Peter 2:9).

All of us are called to praise God with our lips and with our lives. For some, the greatest way to praise God is to offer our lives in Christian ministry. When we make this offer, God will use us — some in a full-time ministry vocation, others in a variety of other ways. A life lived in fellowship with God will be a fruitful one that brings praise and honor to the Lord.

4. The call to suffer. Another universal call, although we may try to avoid it, is the call to suffer.

"How is it to your credit if you receive a beating for doing wrong and endure it? But if you suffer for doing good and you endure it, this is commendable before God. To this you were called, because Christ suffered for you, leaving you an example, that you should follow in his steps" (1 Peter 2:20–21).

Your suffering may come as physical pain. You may suffer financially. You might suffer in struggling with uncertainty about the future or experience the pain of loneliness. Only in God's will can you find contentment and peace, but do not forget that the path of suffering is common to us all.

5. The call to freedom and service. God expects your life to be free from sin. If you do not have the desire to be free from sin and disobedience, it is impossible to minister as God desires.

"It is for freedom that Christ has set us free. Stand firm, then, and do not let yourselves be burdened again by a yoke of slavery. You, my brothers, were called to be free. But do not use your freedom to indulge the sinful nature" (Galatians 5:1, 13).

Self-Evaluation

As you try to discover whether God has called you to specific ministry, you must be obedient to the clear calls the Lord has given.

Ask yourself the following questions regarding these calls:

1. Am I sure I am a Christian? Do I have a personal relationship with the Lord now? Am I walking in fellowship with God on a daily basis? Have I personally invited Christ to be the Lord as well as the Savior of my life?

2. How is my personal holiness? Do I "report for duty" each day to be used in any way God wants? Do I regularly and immediately confess my sin when I commit it? Do I go anywhere, say anything, read or watch anything that would embarrass me if Jesus were to return suddenly? Am I cautious not to grieve the Holy Spirit who lives within me by my words, thoughts, or actions? How obedient am I to this call to holiness?

3. How is my praise of the Lord? Do I spend as much time in praising God as I do in asking the Lord to bless me and mine? Do

I praise God to others? Does my lifestyle bring praise or reproach to the name of God?

4. How do I react when I have to suffer? Do I complain or ask God to remove from me the very thing the Lord may have purposed for my growth? Do I avoid criticism for my Christian faith by keeping silent when I should be speaking up? Do I always want to take the easy way out instead of accepting the difficult assignments God may have placed in my path? Have I learned the secret of "being content in whatever state I am" (Philippians 4:11)?

5. Am I free to enjoy life or am I burdened with legalistic rules and regulations? Am I enjoying my Christianity so much that it is a joy to serve and do anything I can to share my faith? Am I burned out in my service for God, or do I still get personal satisfaction when I do anything in Christ's name and service? Is it a drudgery to obey God's call to holiness? Or have I filled my life so full of God that I don't miss those things others need to be happy?

Notes

1. Henlee H. Barnette, *Has God Called You?* (Nashville: Broadman Press, 1969), 15.

2. Felix E. Montgomery, *Pursuing God's Call: Choosing a Vocation in Ministry* (Nashville: Convention Press, 1981), 15.

3. Barnette, 17.

4. Ibid., 68.

5. Henlee S. Barnette, *Christian Calling and Vocation* (Grand Rapids: Baker Books, 1965), 79.

6. J. Winston Pearce, *God Calls Me* (Nashville: Convention Press, 1960), 47.

7. Franklin M. Segler, *A Theology of Church and Ministry* (Nashville: Broadman Press, 1960), 39.

8. Dennis M. Campbell, *Who Will Go for Us?* (Nashville: Abingdon, 1994), 18.

9. H. Richard Niebuhr, *The Purpose of The Church and Its Ministry* (New York: Harper and Row, 1956), 58.

10. Hugh Thomas Kerr Jr., *A Compend of the Institutes of the Christian Religion* by John Calvin (Philadelphia: Presbyterian Board of Christian Education, 1939), 166.

11. Oswald Chambers, *My Utmost for His Highest: An Updated Version* (Grand Rapids: Discovery House Publishers, 1992), September 29.

12. Ralph H. Elliott, "The Minister as Professional," *Foundations,* 22 (April-June, 1979): 121.

13. Henry Bettensen, ed. *Documents of the Christian Church,* 2nd edition (London: Oxford University Press, 1975), 62–63.

14. E. Glenn Hinson, *The Evangelization of the Roman Empire* (Macon, Ga.: Mercer University Press, 1981), 87–88.

15. Barnette, *Has God Called You?,* 18, 70.

16. Bruce Grubbs, "Making Ministry Full," in *Called to Serve: Ministry for the 21st Century,* Joe R. Stacker, ed. (Nashville: Convention Press, 1993), 12.

17. Richard W. Christopherson, "Calling and Career in Christian Ministry," *Review of Religious Research* 35, No. 3 (March 1, 1994): 224.

18. Ibid., 255.

19. Richard R. Broholm, "How Can You Believe You're a Minister When the Church Keeps Telling You You're Not?" *American Baptist Quarterly* 3, No. 2 (June, 1994): 178–179.

20. William H. Lewis, *The Call to Ministry* (New York: John Trow Printer, 1854), 14.

Chapter Two

EXPERIENCING A CALL TO MINISTRY

"Got a minute, Dr. C.?" he asked, standing in the doorway of my office.

"Sure. Come on in," I replied, as I laid the stack of papers I was grading onto a larger pile of ungraded exams. I wondered what he wanted, hoping I could quickly return to what I had been doing before he arrived.

"I have a question I need some help with," he said, taking his place in the comfortable, stuffed chair sitting beside my desk. "I am having some doubts about what God may be calling me to do."

Immediately I voiced a quick, silent prayer. First, I confessed my temptation to be so busy with my agenda that I was irritated when interrupted. Then, I asked God to give me guidance in helping the student. "Tell me what's been happening," I replied, turning my desk chair so I could face him directly.

"I have always wanted to be a doctor," he said, beginning to spill over with obvious concern and confusion. "I am majoring in pre-med, but lately I have been feeling that God might want me to change to religion and study to become a preacher. I know I could serve the Lord as a Christian doctor. I am just not sure what to do."

I walked over to my office door to close it, trying to eliminate any distractions from the office suite. I sensed that this "interruption" was one that had long-range implications.

"I am planning on going on a mission trip to India next

month," he shared. "Perhaps God will use that trip to help me understand his will for me."

I encouraged him to talk about what he had been feeling and shared with him some things that had been helpful to me when trying to discern how God leads. We prayed together before he left the office, and I assured him I would be praying for him as he continued to seek God's will about his choice of major and future vocation.

A few months passed. One day he peeked his head into my office, and with a big smile on his face, he reported, "God touched my heart while I was in India. Sign me up to be a religion major," he said, with obvious joy on his face and in his tone of voice. "It's truly great to know that God has called me into vocational Christian ministry."

Over the past twenty-three years, many students have come to my office to share with me their call experiences. Some know that God has called them to a specific ministry. Others are seeking clarification regarding the particulars of their call or simply for support in making a vocational decision.

You may be wondering if God is calling you to some special work or ministry in the kingdom. You may be confused about an experience you've had that you think may be a call of some kind. You may have responded to what you thought was a call to ministry only to doubt its validity and desire clarification. Perhaps you are seeking help in counseling others who are struggling with the issue of calling to ministry. Whatever your reason for reading this book, it is my prayer that God will grant you the understanding you seek.

> Each person recognizes God's call in his or her life through his or her own unique circumstances. For some it is at the right time and in the way that can be responded to by curiosity. For others it is at the right time and in a way that they need help in clarifying the call. God still speaks to us today and the call is present in today's world.... Discerning the action required of God's call in vocation requires further listening and conversation with God.[1]

As a part of the research for writing this book, I conducted a survey with people who say they have experienced a call to ministry. One of the questions I asked the 365 participants was whether they would consider their call (1) one that was a gradual, growing conviction that the Lord was leading in that direction, or (2) a specific call at a time and place they could recall. Sixty-six percent said their calls were gradual, while only 33 percent said their calls were sudden or occurred at a time they could pinpoint. This may be encouraging to many of you who have the impression that a call must be dramatic and specific before it is genuine.

What Does a Call to Ministry Involve?

It was in February, while I was riding on an old dirt road. God and I were having a talk. As I was doing the talking, God's presence came all over me, and I had to stop talking and start listening. [The Lord] impressed upon my heart that my name was written in the Lamb's Book of Life. I was overwhelmed, but that was not all that God wanted me to hear. The power of God was still with me, as I began to weep. . . . I asked [God], "What else am I to do?" Right then in my heart was the message, "Go forth and preach the gospel."

Such was the written testimony of one of the students at Fruitland Bible Institute. This is the kind of testimony many people expect to hear from a person who has experienced a call to ministry. While many people do experience such a "clarion" call, many others testify that their calls were not as dramatic but just as certain. Consider the testimony of another Fruitland Bible Institute student:

My calling really began when I went on a mission trip with a church group from my church. It was my first mission trip, and God really worked in my life that week. As I reached out to help others, it seemed God was reaching back to me with blessings far more than I had given out. During that week, God began to show me that there was something missing in my life, I was just not doing all [the Lord] wanted me to do. At that time, I didn't understand all that was going on, and it wasn't until two years later that God revealed to me that [the Lord] wanted me in missions full time, not just one week a year.

Another person shares this call experience: "I have always been in church, as far back as I can remember. Anytime there was something going on at church, I was there. I can remember many of the older adult ladies in the church telling me I 'would make a good preacher one day.' Serving God and the church have always been such a big part of my life, it just seems like I have grown into the call."

Sudden calls; gradual calls. Calls accepted easily; calls from which the person runs. Calls that come directly from an encounter with God; calls discovered through the counsel of others. Such are the testimonies of multitudes who have followed what they considered to be the Lord's call into vocational Christian ministry. Listen to the call experiences of others, some recorded in recent history, others in the Scripture. The experiences may parallel your own and give you the assurance you need to continue in the direction you are headed.

In Recent History

Teacher and Missionary to China[2]

Charlotte "Lottie" Moon was the fourth of seven children, born in a country home in Virginia to well-to-do parents. Her mother and father were strong Christians, active in their church. Often they would open their house to traveling missionaries who were at home on furlough.

Her mother often read to the children stories about missionaries, a favorite being the story of Ann Judson, the first Baptist woman missionary from America.

When Lottie was ten years old, her uncle answered the call to become a missionary in Israel. Lottie, however, began to develop a strong hostility toward Christianity and avoided the church whenever possible. When she left home to attend boarding school, she impressed her teachers with her intelligence, but her family and friends were anxious about her apparent lack of concern for her spiritual condition.

Some time later, during a series of evangelistic meetings at the church near the school, Lottie made a public profession of her faith in Jesus and applied for membership in the church. The pastor there made a constant appeal to the student members for a life commitment to religious work. God's hand was on this young lady, calling her to missions, although many years would pass before that call would be realized.

Charlotte became a teacher, but God kept the fires of missions burning in her heart through the letters of a sister who went to China as a missionary and wrote home of the great needs for laborers. One morning when her pastor was preaching a sermon on the need for laborers in the vineyard, Charlotte left her front-row pew to pray in her room all afternoon. Later she told her pastor that his sermon had cemented her determination to go to China. She told others that she "heard her call to China as clear as a bell." On July 7, 1873, Charlotte "Lottie" Moon was officially appointed a missionary of the Southern Baptist Foreign Mission Board in Richmond and was commissioned to go to Tengchow, China.

The Making of a Crusader[3]

"How could a shy, Carolina country boy be transformed into a global ambassador for the Kingdom of Heaven?" asked the writer of his autobiography. He was reared in a Christian home with parents who loved him and believed in "training up a child in the way he should go." He was energetic and mischievous, sometimes causing his family great concern. Once his mother took him to the doctor and exclaimed, "He just isn't normal. He's got too much energy. He never runs down."

As a growing boy, he was filled with self-doubt. Even as a teenager, he was afraid to attend youth meetings for fear he would be called upon to testify. His school teachers knew he was shy, and he was obviously embarrassed that he was a foot taller than his classmates. While he seemed indifferent, and his grades were unusually low, some of his teachers noticed a "slumbering potential which would burst forth occasionally." This tongue-tied country boy would grow up to become a religious statesman, a worldwide evangelist, a "fluent, powerful orator." What could have happened to cause such an unusual transformation?

He joined his parents' church when he was twelve but did not make a personal commitment of his life to God until he was sixteen. He was convicted and converted at an area-wide crusade, not realizing one day that his name would become almost synonymous with the word "crusade."

He completed high school and entered college. He dropped out but later enrolled at Florida Bible Institute. During one of the services for the student body, the speaker issued a challenge for the students to give themselves completely to God's service. The young man burst from the assembly, knowing he must make a decision. "I had fought that call for weeks," he said. "I remember sitting... looking up at the moon and the stars. A soft breeze was sweeping in from the south. I recall getting down on my knees and saying, 'O God, if you want me to preach, I will do it.' Tears were streaming down my cheeks as I made the great surrender to become an ambassador for Christ."

Only time and eternity will reveal the impact of that decision for the Kingdom of God made that day by Billy Graham.

A Prince of Preachers[4]

The Baptist church at Whitewright, Texas, soon discovered the teaching and speaking talents of the congenial young man who had joined their church. Before long they asked him to serve as their superintendent of Sunday school. And when the pastor was absent, they asked him to preach at the worship hour. The young man had such respect for the ordained ministry that he stood down in front of the pulpit when he was invited to substitute for the pastor. He had no aspirations to become a minister, desiring instead to become a lawyer.

Gradually, however, the members of that little church became convinced that this young man should be a preacher. Individuals and groups in the church discussed their convictions, and some talked with the young man about the idea. He responded each time by saying, "I am perfectly willing to talk for Christ, but not from a pulpit."

One night during a church conference, one of the oldest deacons rose to his feet to make the following motion: "I move that
this church call a presbytery to ordain Brother George W. Truett
to the full gospel ministry." Although he appealed to them to
wait at least six months and talk it over, they said, "Brother
George, we have a deep conviction that you ought to be preaching. We won't wait six months; we won't wait six hours. We are
called to do this now, and we are going ahead with it. We are
moved by a deep conviction that it is the will of God. We dare
not wait. We must follow our convictions."

Before the night had passed, fighting a fierce inner battle,
George W. Truett's mind and heart surrendered to the call to
preach the gospel of Jesus Christ. Little did he know that, for
more than a generation, he would serve as pastor of First Baptist
Church in Dallas, Texas, one of the nation's greatest churches,
and that he would be regarded as the outstanding Baptist leader
in Texas and one of the most effective preachers of his century.

In Biblical History

Some of the most well-known biblical calls are those experienced
by Abraham (Genesis 12), Moses (Exodus 3), Jonah (Jonah 1–4),
Isaiah (Isaiah 6), and Saul/Paul (Acts 9). A careful study of their
experiences may help you clarify some things, but be cautious.
Don't assume from these examples that a call must be dramatic
or sudden for it to be genuine.

Throughout the Old Testament, the Lord called the nation of
Israel to relationship and service. But God also called individuals,
men and women alike. Abraham was called to be the father of
the nation. Moses, Aaron, and Miriam were chosen to lead Israel
out of bondage in Egypt. Isaiah, Jeremiah, Deborah, Ezekiel, Elijah, and a host of others were commissioned to speak to, warn,
and minister to God's people.

Samuel was a young boy when God called him to serve. "The
call came in the quietness of the night, quietly but with increas-
ing clarity."[5] God called Ruth to "become an alien refugee for
the sake of love."[6] Joshua was eighty when God asked him to

lead the nation of Israel into the promised land. When Jeremiah received his call, he begged for release because the "burden of preaching with integrity was so crushing."[7] God called Amos to leave sheep herding to become a spokesman to a wayward nation. God called Deborah, a prophetess, judge, and hymnodist, to fill a major role in the deliverance of Israel. "Hers was a ministry of the word of God, expressed in sermon, song, and counsel."[8] God used Hosea and his failing marriage to speak to the adulterous nation of Israel. In the crisis in the days of King Josiah, the prophetess Huldah was consulted as an authority on the Law and the word of God. She was "the dominant figure in the reforms around 640 B.C."[9] Esther was called to "exercise wisdom, cunning and power for the sake of a people."[10]

God also used priests, prophets, and scribes who were closely connected with the temple, the official community of faith. By the time of Elijah and Elisha, disciples of the prophets had organized into bodies called the "sons of the prophets." During the days of Isaiah tradition set apart a group of disciples whose responsibility was to proclaim, interpret, and apply the prophets' words to the nation.

Throughout the New Testament, God continued to call people into a relationship with their Creator through Jesus. All believers were commissioned to reach the entire world, making disciples of those who answered the call to salvation. But God also called individuals to specific ministries, to carry out given tasks within the overall plan of reaching the world.

Mary, betrothed of Joseph and while yet a virgin, was called to bear the Son of God. Jesus chose the Twelve to walk in a closeness of relationship and service that others were not privileged to have. A concerned brother influenced the skeptical Peter and led him to answer the call to salvation, leaving behind his boat and nets in order to follow Christ. Peter went on to experience other "calls" to service as he continued to follow that original summons to become a fisher of men and women. Saul of Tarsus experienced a dramatic call to service that involved a personal transformation and a change of his very name; he became Paul, the great apostle to the Gentiles. Apparently the Lord led

Timothy into service through the influence of a godly home and the tutelage of his mother and grandmother. Paul took Titus and Timothy under his wing, helping them first develop as disciples of the Lord and then as ministers of the gospel.

As a young man, Mark was influenced by his relative Barnabas, who invited him to be a part of a ministry endeavor and who stood by him even when Mark failed. Aquila and Priscilla served as a team in ministry, supporting themselves by tent making. Phoebe was a deaconess. The four daughters of Philip prophesied.

Common Elements of a Call to Ministry

While reading the call experiences included in this book, you probably noticed one thing in particular: they were all different. Just as our conversion experiences differ, so do our call experiences. Avoid the temptation of thinking your experience has to be like someone else's to be valid. The Lord will work with you in a unique way. You must be obedient to what God shows *you.*

Having said that, however, I must add that most call experiences share some common elements. Consider whether you have experienced any of the following:

1. A restlessness with what one is doing at present. This may be a dissatisfaction with your current vocation or just a desire to be doing more for God. You may feel drawn toward a certain ministry you see someone else performing. You may experience a strong desire to serve a specific group of people or feel a burning desire to fill a particular need. But a common theme expressed by many who have felt and followed a call to ministry is this restlessness in their lives.

One word of caution at this point. Restlessness can be caused by situations other than a call to the ministry. Dissatisfaction with our current lot in life may be prompted by God because of sin, disobedience, or a failure to use our spiritual gifts. Alternatively, being stuck in a job that is unrewarding or an unpleasant relationship and enduring various other physical, social, and personal problems can also cause a restlessness in our lives. If, however, we examine all of these areas and eliminate any rest-lessness derived from them, then we should seriously consider that God may be calling us to serve in a special way.

2. An inner tug or word from God. The still, small voice of conviction is difficult to explain, but it brings a certainty that *this* is what we must do. You may sense that a certain direction is right, and when you walk in that direction, you experience personal satisfaction and peace. That feeling of fulfillment is hard to describe, but in your heart you know you are where you should be. You have an assurance, even in the face of difficulties or opposition, that you are doing the right thing.

3. Confirmation from others in the community of faith. When you begin to follow the call of God, some confirmation may come from the encouragement of more mature believers who see the spark of God in your life. You will begin to see doors open for you to exercise the ministry to which you feel led. Other people might express appreciation for your ministry or service, and you will see fruit from your labors. Later you might receive formal support in the shape of election to leadership positions or via the more formal method of ordination. Assurance will come as you continue to walk one step at a time on your spiritual journey.

But What about Me?

Perhaps you have identified with some of these experiences and with those described in the preceding testimonies. Still, you may be confused about how to hear God speak. Remember that often God's voice comes as an inward tug, a stirring within the very heart of a person. At other times the Spirit impresses our minds with a need and then gives us the desire to meet that need. Do you remember how you felt when God convicted you of your sins and you became a Christian? God's call to ministry may come to you in a similar way. Don't stumble over the misconception that you must literally "hear" the audible voice of God before you respond. Jesus says that his sheep will know his voice (John 10). Conviction of God's call may come as a thought in your mind or as a pounding of your heart as you consider the Lord's will for you. Don't shut down your mind, and don't be afraid of your feelings either.

We will talk more about the will of God and how to discern a call in Chapter Three. For now, commit your life to God and wait for the Lord's will to be made clear to you. If you are not sure you are willing to follow wherever God leads, ask the Spirit to make you willing. The Lord will faithfully answer the prayers of a sincere, seeking heart.

Wait for the Wind

My nephew's ten-year-old son, Tripper, came for a visit one hot July weekend. I was enticing him to stay inside by joining him in a video game, but after being defeated mercilessly by a more experienced player, I suggested that we take a break for a while. I collapsed into my favorite recliner to let my neck muscles relax and my ego recover from such a beating. Tripper slipped out of the room, and I caught a few relished moments of peace and quiet.

"Look, Alice," he said enthusiastically as he ran over to the chair where I was recovering. "I found a kite. Could we go outside and fly it?"

Glancing out a nearby window, I noticed not a breeze was stirring. "I'm sorry, Tripper," I said, sad to see his disappointed eyes but secretly thankful for the respite from more activity. "The wind isn't blowing today. The kite won't fly."

The determined young boy replied. "I think it's windy enough. I can get it to fly," he answered, as he hurried out the back door.

I peeked through the slats in the Venetian blinds to watch his determination in action. Up and down the yard he ran, pulling the kite attached to a small length of string. The plastic kite, proudly displaying a picture of Batman, remained at about shoulder level. He ran back and forth, as fast as his ten-year-old legs would carry him, looking back hopefully at the kite trailing behind.

After about ten minutes, he came back in. I asked, "How did it go?"

"Fine," he said, not wanting to admit defeat. "I got it to fly some."

As he walked past me to return the kite to the closet shelf, I heard him say under his breath, "I guess I'll have to wait for the wind."

At that moment I heard another Voice speak to my heart. "Alice, sometimes you are just like that. You want to do it your way instead of waiting for my Wind."

How true! We prefer to use our own efforts to accomplish what we want to do. We wait for the Wind only after we have done all we can, exhausting our own strength. We must learn how to rely on the Spirit's wind in the first place!

Perhaps you are running from a call to ministry, afraid of what that call will mean for you. Or maybe you're struggling to hear God's calling for your life. After asking every question and trying every trick, you may remain confused and exhausted. Perhaps the difficulty is in your unwillingness to wait for the Wind, to wait until God is ready to make the call clear to you. Be assured that, wherever you are in your spiritual journey, God wants to speak to you and will do so at the right time.

> Free will is like the sailor adjusting tiller and sheets. Though it is sometimes a struggle, we can choose to hold the boat of our life steady into the wind of the Spirit. Then our efforts are sup-ported and directed by grace. One caution. Once we have opened our sails to that wind, we need to be prepared to go where the Spirit blows. — Saint Anselm

Are you open to the call of God on your life? Ask yourself the following questions, and discuss your responses with a mature Christian who knows you and whom you trust.

Attitude

What is your attitude toward the idea of a unique calling from God? How open are you to the possibility of pursuing full-time vocational ministry? Are you willing to leave people, places, and things to follow wherever God leads and to do whatever God asks? Have you considered how following God's call will affect your family? Are you willing to follow God, even if you cannot see where the journey will take you? How confident are you that the Lord will bless you as you walk in obedience to this special calling? Are you restless in your current situation? Is that restlessness a symptom of your impatience or dissatisfaction, or do you sense the Spirit moving in your heart to ready you for a change? Are you content to "wait for the Wind" and to serve God where you are until the Spirit's calling is made clear to you?

Practical Considerations and Potential Obstacles

Have you considered what might present an obstacle to your following God's will and fulfilling God's purpose in ministry? What worries you about pursuing God's call for your life? Are you concerned about your age — that you are too old or too young to answer the call? Do you feel inadequate to live up to God's calling — whether because of low self-esteem, lack of education, limited experience, or an awareness of your own sinfulness? Do questions and doubts paralyze your response to the call? What uncertainties haunt you, and what can you do to feel more secure about your sense of calling? Have you considered your family background and prayed about what experiences you have had that might hinder your ability to serve God and others with humility and compassion? Following God's call often gives rise to opposition from family and friends who do not know Christ; do you recognize who in your life might react negatively to a decision to enter full-time vocational ministry? What grounds — legitimate or imagined — might they have for objecting? How will you resist those objections and overcome the obstacles when they arise? What aspects of your own lifestyle might be in conflict with total obedience to God? What behaviors or choices in companions could prove to be stumbling blocks for those whom you want to serve? Is it possible that God has already spoken to you but that you are fleeing from the Spirit's call? If so, why are you running?

Preparation

How long have you been a Christian? When did you first sense a special calling from God on your life? How has God spoken to you in the past? Are you aware of how God has moved in your life previously so you can be more sensitive to the Lord's working now and in the future? Have you reflected upon your experiences to date and considered what lessons God has been teaching you through the storms? How might those lessons contribute to your readiness for vocational ministry? What unusual experiences have you had? Have you considered what God might be trying to communicate to you through those experiences? Have you evaluated your own gifts and talents and surrendered them to the Lord? Are you aware of the needs in people and circumstances around you? Do you recognize suffering in others and long to reach out with compassion to those who are hurting? What kind of ministry experience do you have? Are you willing to volunteer in various capacities so that God may use you as the Spirit sees fit?

Spiritual Growth and Maturity

Are you satisfied with your present relationship with God? Why or why not? Are there areas in your spiritual development that cause you concern, where you need to trust more, or where you need to seek God's forgiveness and cleansing? How would you characterize your relationship with God? Does an encounter with the Spirit leave you humbled, chastened, broken, exhilarated, joyful, awed, comforted? What about *you* determines the nature of that encounter? Have you cultivated a posture of humility and obedience, a willingness to do what God asks promptly and without question? When you do have questions, what do you ask? Do you expect God to speak to you through life's circumstances? Are you open to hearing God speak through the voices of other people? How open are you to correction — through Scripture, through experience, and through the wise counsel of others? Are you willing to test your convictions by seeking advice and confirmation from mature Christians whom you trust? Are you able to confess your desires and expectations to God and then leave them with the Lord, accepting that what you want and what God actually does may be two different things? Do you trust God to work through you and your ministry, even if what you hope to see does not come to pass?

Notes

1. Ray Lewis, *Choosing Your Career, Finding Your Vocation* (New York: Paulist Press, 1989), 39.

2. Catherine B. Allen, *The New Lottie Moon Story* (Nashville: Broadman Press, 1980).

3. Curtis Mitchell, *The Making of a Crusader* (Philadelphia: Chilton Books, 1966).

4. P. W. James, *George W. Truett, A Biography* (New York: The Macmillan Company, 1945).

5. Frank Stagg, "Understanding Call to Ministry," in *Formation for Christian Ministry,* Davis and Rowett, eds. (Louisville: Southern Baptist Seminary, 1988), 39.

6. Richard Carlson, "Not Choosing, but Being Chosen," *The Christian Ministry* (January-February, 1994): 10.

7. Stagg, 41.

8. Ibid., 40.

9. Ibid., 41.

10. Carlson, 10.

Chapter Three

DISCERNING GOD'S CALL TO MINISTRY

"I think God may want me to go to the foreign mission field, but I am not sure."

"I am not sure how you can know whether your thoughts are from God or just your own."

"I hear people say that God spoke to them, but I am not sure I have ever had that experience. They talk like they heard an audible voice."

For many years now, I have heard sincere people raise these same questions. When we earnestly want to understand and do God's will, we soon realize how difficult it is to know for certain when God is calling us to a specific task. There are no easy answers, but the Bible does give some guidelines to help.

God speaks through Scripture as it is energized by the Holy Spirit who lives in our hearts. The importance of reading, studying, and meditating on God's Word cannot be overemphasized. The Christian who is earnestly seeking to know and do the will of God must be a student of the Word of God. The Spirit will faithfully reveal divine truths to us as we read and study the Bible — the standard by which we must judge all decisions, the anchor that holds us when we are faltering, the lamp that illumines, the sword that convicts, and the food that nourishes.

You may wonder what biblical passages you should read when you are seeking God's will about something. I would encourage you to read the Bible on a daily basis, not just when you are looking for an answer to a particular problem. You should store

Scripture in your mind so the Holy Spirit will have a reservoir from which to select verses when you need them.

A case in point: I always begin my classes at the university with a few Bible verses, a short devotion, and prayer. Each morning I seek the Lord's direction regarding the verses I should share. One morning about two years ago, certain verses from John 14 kept coming to mind.

> Do not let your hearts be troubled. Trust in God; trust also in me. In my Father's house are many rooms; if it were not so, I would have told you. I am going there to prepare a place for you. And if I go and prepare a place for you, I will come back and take you to be with me that you also may be where I am. (John 14:1–3)

I tried to replace these verses with others, deciding these were not really appropriate for the students that morning. I was worried they might wonder why I was sharing a text that is often used at funerals! I couldn't get the words out of my mind, however, so I decided to share them. I concluded that someone in the class might be facing a difficulty in which such verses would be helpful.

Later that day when I was at home cooking supper, the phone rang. It was my brother. "Alice," he said, "I have some bad news. Mom died this afternoon." Immediately I knew why the Lord had placed those verses from John 14 on my heart that morning. God knew that I was the one who would need them that day!

The Lord has graciously provided the Scriptures for us and desires to speak to us through them, but we must read, study, and meditate upon the Bible on a daily basis if we want to benefit from the treasures God has placed within it.

God speaks through prayer. We were discussing this topic one day in class, and one student asked the crucial question of *how.* "If I am talking to God, how can God be talking to me at the same time?"

You may have wondered the same thing: "I can understand how important it is for me to pray about God's will for me, but I don't understand how God speaks to *me* when I pray." Some of the difficulty may arise when we fail to define the nature of prayer. Prayer is communicating with God, but that doesn't mean we should do all the talking! Good communication involves listening as well, and perhaps that is our greatest weakness. We know how to talk, but we aren't very good listeners.

Henry Blackaby reminds us that "prayer is designed more to adjust you to God than to adjust God to you."[1] As we spend time with God, especially when we are "listening" for that still, small voice, the Lord can speak to us, guiding us in our current circumstances or giving us direction for a future assignment. Our job is to listen; God's responsibility is to speak.

God speaks through circumstances to guide us. Open and closed doors of opportunity are some of those circumstantial methods. Paul told the church at Corinth that he planned to "stay on at Ephesus until Pentecost, because a great door for effective work has opened to me" (1 Corinthians 16:8–9). Later he asked the Colossians to "pray for us, too, that God may open a door for our message, so that we may proclaim the mystery of Christ" (Colossians 4:3).

We should *develop the habit of looking for the doors of opportunity* God opens for us each day to serve. When we walk faithfully through those doors, we are more likely to be where God wants us when we have to make major decisions about our lives. Keep in mind, however, that although God does use open and closed doors to guide us, sometimes a door that seems open may be closed and vice versa. Pray as you walk in the direction you think God is leading and try to go through the door that seems to be opening.

Ask others to help you discern possible doors. Proverbs 11:14 advises that "in the multitude of counselors there is safety." When we talk with other Christians and ask their guidance, God often uses them to help us see things we may not see otherwise. Since we are all members of the body of Christ, it is not less "spiritual" for God to speak through someone else who is a member of the body! One word of caution: be certain the advice from others coincides with your own impressions as you study God's Word and pray.

Talk to people who know the church or institution you are

considering. Ask family and friends who know your strengths and weaknesses whether they think you are equipped for the ministry you are considering. Although the final word of direction must come from God, the Spirit often uses others to help us discern God's will.

Be realistic about what you expect God to do and what you should do for yourself. Sometimes God leads us with no assistance from us. At other times we need to send out resumés, talk to friends, or do something else to help a door open. Don't limit God to only one way of leading you.

Don't force a door to open. Wait for God's timing. God may show you a certain door through which you will pass one day, but you can complicate the issue by running ahead. When multiple doors of opportunity appear open, rely on prayer, meditation on the Scriptures, and support of godly friends to help you discern the will of God. Gather as much information as you can about the opportunities and yourself, and pray for peace as you try to discern where God is leading.

God also works through the circumstances of our own interests and abilities. God made us and often works with our interests and abilities to accomplish divine purposes through us. God does not expect us to do something we have not been equipped to do. While our natural interests and abilities are not the only way God works, we would be wrong not to consider them in the general scheme of things.

Moreover, we must not forget that *God has given us minds to use.* Sometimes sanctified common sense can be very useful when discerning God's will. God is not unreasonable in the Spirit's calling. If I can't carry a tune in a bucket, God is unlikely to lead me to become a minister of music!

One morning, in discussing the topic of God's leadership, I commented to one of my university classes that many people have the mistaken idea that if they hate something, *that* is the very thing God will want them to do. I mentioned that a person who hates to study and prepare sermons should seriously consider that dislike as an indication that God is probably *not* calling him or her to be a preacher.

Later that day, one of the students came to my office and shared with me that God had spoken to him through my words in class. He said he didn't like school and really wanted to be a farmer. He had come to school following what he had thought was a call to preach. The more we talked, the more he realized he had misunderstood the situation. A great sense of peace came over him as he realized God's will for him also happened to be what he most wanted to do! As you may have heard, "Don't necessarily think that the 'G.P.' you see written in the clouds means 'Go Preach.' It may mean 'Go Plow!'"

On the other hand, what we consider reasonable and preferable may *not* be what God has planned. God may want us to preach when we think we would rather plow. The Lord can take a vessel that seems unproductive and make it a mighty instrument in service. Using our common sense, however, is one way we look for what God is doing in our lives. As we become more aware of ourselves and all that concerns us, we are more likely to see the hand of God at work around us. God works in harmony with our abilities, interests, talents, and spiritual gifts, as well as within the personal desires and aspirations that are already in our minds. At the same time, we must take care that all of our desires are under Christ's lordship. Everyone I know who is busy doing God's will is extremely happy, whether in a "sacred" or "secular" calling — even when called upon to do unpleasant things that may go along with the job. If God does call us to what some fear most: "remaining single, going to Africa, and eating grasshoppers," we may be confident that it will be a delightful experience — because we are where God has called us to be.

God speaks through our spiritual gifts. One way we may begin to understand God's call for our lives is to consider the spiritual gifts we possess.

"I believe I was passed over when God was giving out spiritual gifts," a young male student blurted out in class one day during our discussion on discovering spiritual gifts. He laughed a bit uncomfortably, and a few of his classmates chuckled along with him. I smiled and suggested he wait until we completed our study before he drew his final conclusions.

Perhaps you have thought the same thing, that you are one God forgot when dispensing gifts. Or you may believe you have at least one spiritual gift but have been unable to discern exactly what it is. Or you may wonder how spiritual gifts and natural talents relate to each other and/or to a call to ministry.

Chapter Four will discuss this subject in more detail, but for now, understand that spiritual gifts are given by the Holy Spirit to the believer. A gift sometimes coincides with or complements a talent, but it is not the same as a talent. Unlike many of our talents, we do not inherit spiritual gifts from our parents. Because spiritual gifts are supernatural — meaning that they are manifestations of the presence of the Holy Spirit in our lives — when we use them, the results will be supernatural. For instance, a beautiful song sung by a talented person will impress us, but a song sung by a person with equal talent coupled with the gift of encouragement will inspire and change us. A talent is a gift *from* God, our Creator; a spiritual gift is a quality that derives from the very nature *of* God. Ask God to reveal to you your spiritual gifts and how they relate to the Spirit's call on your life.

God also speaks through inner impressions, that still small voice within our own hearts. This mode of divine communication is sometimes more difficult to discern than the other methods I have mentioned, but it is important nonetheless. Consider the scriptural witness to the reality:

> Whether you turn to the right or to the left, your ears will hear a voice behind you, saying, "This is the way; walk in it" (Isaiah 30:21).

> Paul and his companions traveled throughout the region of Phrygia and Galatia, having been kept by the Holy Spirit from preaching the word in the province of Asia. When they came to the border of Mysia, they tried to enter Bithynia, but the Spirit of Jesus would not allow them to. (Acts 16:6–7)

> After the wind there was an earthquake, but the LORD was not in the earthquake. After the earthquake came a fire, but the LORD was not in the fire. And after the fire came a gentle whisper. (1 Kings 19:11b–12)

How do we explain how we know when God calls us to act? It is as difficult as explaining how we were convicted of our need for salvation or how we knew when God's Spirit entered our hearts. But the assurance of those events is real. More than likely, anyone who has felt and answered some call will tell you "you'll just know" when God speaks. That offers little comfort, however, when you are trying to *know* for yourself!

Some principles may help you as you try to determine if God is speaking to you about a call to ministry — or any other aspect of the Lord's will for you.

God does not drive us; God leads us. The compulsion to do something for God is a strong, underlying conviction, not an impulsive, hurried decision; an invitation, not a demand; a call, not an ultimatum. The Lord speaks to us in gentle but clear ways.

God gives us time to test the genuineness of our impressions. Time will help the Spirit's impressions grow stronger. Selfish impulses grow weaker as we pray and follow God. If we become impulsive, we are likely to make costly mistakes. Too often we ask God something and then go ahead and do what we want to before the Lord answers!

Impressions from God welcome the light of inquiry. God delights in having us talk with other believers and ask for their prayers and wisdom. Gather as much information as possible concerning the decision you are trying to make. If you are considering a certain vocation, talk with those who are serving in that ministry. Ask them to share both the good and the bad parts of the job. You might even ask if you can follow them around for a few weeks, observing the ministry roles they fill.

Do not rely too heavily on feelings. Learn how to distinguish between a feeling and a conviction from God. Feelings are unreliable, being affected by your physical condition, state of mind, and even the weather. Feelings often fluctuate over time and are easily influenced by what others think or by changing circumstances. Our feelings tend to push us to make hurried decisions without seeking wise counsel or taking the time to gather information or to ponder consequences. On the other hand, a conviction from God is constant; it allows time for honest reflection, and it gladly accepts wisdom from others who are more mature in their faith and spiritual understanding.

As you continue to grow as a Christian, you will find it easier to differentiate between your feelings and a true conviction from God.

Do not use random biblical texts to confirm God's voice. If you simply open the Bible at random and point to a verse expecting divine revelation, you are deceiving yourself. Study the Bible to get a clear understanding of God's will and of how God communicates that will to human beings. As you become familiar with biblical truths and practice obedience in all areas of your Christian life, you will be more open to the "specifics" God wants to reveal. People who are most prone to the "chance Bible text" trap are those who don't want to take the time and effort to study the Bible, which is a lifelong task.

Don't let your imagination run wild. You can talk yourself into believing almost anything. Be careful that you are not simply painting an idea in your mind that you hope is God's will for you.

Don't rely too heavily on dreams. Dreams can originate from a variety of sources, including the pizza you ate before going to bed! Place more confidence in the ways God speaks to you when you are awake. This is not to say that God will never speak to you through a dream, but Scripture and the wise counsel of others are more reliable channels through which the Holy Spirit works.

Be careful about "putting out the fleece." Although that test was appropriate for Gideon, who did not have the indwelling Holy Spirit or the written Word of God, this approach is one filled with dangers for us. Too many things can happen coincidentally. And, aren't we a bit presumptuous and immature to expect God to speak according to our dictates before we will believe? We are wise to look for open and closed doors, but playing the game of "signs and wonders" is dangerous and potentially misleading.

Be prepared for surprises. At times God will speak when you least expect it. Always try to be open and ready to hear the Lord speak. God's call to teach came to me as I sat listening to a sermon about giving to the building fund! Perhaps that was the only time I was quiet enough in the midst of my busy schedule for the Spirit to get a message through to me.

Be humble before the Lord. Confess your confusion and need for clear direction. Do not be embarrassed about the uncertainty in your life when you are face-to-face with the One whose will you seek to know. God may be waiting for you to come as a child and simply ask.

As you try to discern the voice of God in a matter, tell the Lord how much you long to be obedient to the Spirit's leading. Begin to walk in the direction you think God is calling you, and ask the Lord either to convict you or to give you peace. God has promised to lead us, but do not insist on complete understanding before taking the next step (Psalm 32:8).

The Will of God and the Call to Ministry

The call to ministry falls within the overall scope of knowing and doing the will of God. Before pursuing a sense of special call-ing, you need a clear idea of how to know the will of God in a general sense. One of the most important things to grasp is an understanding of "the will of God," which may best be defined as "the personal intent or purpose which God desires or wishes."[2] The idea always implies a personal relationship with God be-cause God's will is never simply a legalistic or rigid plan we try to follow. Many people who are trying to know and do God's will misunderstand this very point and therefore experience great difficulty.

Although we all want God to give us a plan all at once, such a desire does not really honor God, who wants to walk with us in a daily relationship, not just give us marching orders to follow. Our lives will be transformed if we stop asking for the package plan and determine to walk with God every day of our lives, even if that decision means we can't see very far down the road.

Prerequisites for Knowing God's Will

If you are willing to make the commitment and take the risk of following God daily, without a blueprint for the future, then you should understand some fundamental principles essential to knowing and following God's will as the Spirit reveals it.

First of all, you must *be a child of God,* one who possesses the Holy Spirit who teaches us all things (John 14:26). Then you must *be willing* to do God's will even before that will is revealed to you (John 7:17). A sure way to remain out of God's will is to insist upon knowing what God desires before we will consent to do it. A willing heart is the key to unlock many closed doors.

Seek to do God's will as Jesus did (John 5:30). Many questions about God's will can be answered by the Scriptures. Read the Gospels regularly and learn how Jesus acted and reacted during his earthly life and ministry.

Pray to know God's will, and do not just try to figure it out for yourself (Psalm 143:10). Those of us who enjoy solving puzzles may get trapped by trying to figure out the pieces of the puzzle of God's will without consulting the Lord who is the ultimate Puzzle Solver. Or perhaps you are among those who are tempted to talk more with others than with God. Remember that the Spirit wants to reveal God's will even more than you want to discover it; if you ask God first, the pieces of the puzzle will certainly fall into place.

Pray that others find God's will as well (Colossians 4:12). Prayer unleashes the power of God in the world. When we pray for others and they for us, the Spirit is free to work in all of us and in our circumstances to clearly lead and use us.

Study God's Word because Scripture is a primary way God speaks to us (Psalm 119:105). Without daily reading and meditation on the Word of God, you will not understand the daily will of God, much less the Lord's larger plan for your life.

Be dedicated to God and not conformed to the world's standards (Romans 12:1–2). Often confusion develops when we try to follow the Lord's standards and those of the world simultaneously. While the world says that money, family, and friends are primary considerations, God may be trying to tell you otherwise by leading you to a certain vocation that involves sacrifice of those very things.

Do not be reluctant but do the Lord's will from the heart (Ephesians 6:6). The attitude you have when you submit to the Lord's will is important. Have you ever obeyed a parent's instruction to do an unpleasant chore with great reluctance and a very negative disposition? Be careful not to obey the Lord with such reluctance or negativity.

Practice obedience in the daily matters of life if you want to know God's will for bigger decisions. Because God's will is a process, you need to shoulder the cross daily (Luke 9:23); that daily commitment should include Bible reading (Acts 17:11), praise and thanksgiving (1 Thessalonians 5:18), self-denial (1 Corinthians 15:31b), prayer (Matthew 6:11), and recognition of God's sovereign control (James 4:13–15). You will encounter extreme difficulty in understanding God's will in major decisions of life if you are not concerned with pursuing the Lord's purposes on a daily basis.

Some Guiding Principles

Although much of God's will is clearly established in the Bible, other aspects of the divine will concern us personally, especially with regard to an individual's call to ministry. Here are some guidelines/principles that will be helpful in understanding those more personal callings.

Realize that *the Spirit gives us the motivation to do God's will* (Philippians 2:13). Be thankful for the very desire to know and to do God's will because that desire in itself is confirmation that the Lord is at work within you. What is more, God will give you what you need to carry out the divine calling (Hebrews 13:20–21).

Since God provides the motivation and the means, all the Lord requires from you is obedience. *God wants your cooperation* to work with and not against the Spirit. Unfortunately humanity tends to struggle with guessing God's will instead of cooperating with what the Lord has already revealed. Struggle to work *with* the Lord because it is *natural* to work against God. As a result, you will need to work constantly to cooperate with what the Spirit of God wants to do in and through you. The watchword of "obedience" is critical in pursuing God's purposes.

Commit to the Lord all that concerns you. When you allow God to be Lord of everything, you will not find it so difficult to determine what God wants for your life's vocation. You *do* need to think, reason, and plan, but be assured of God's guidance in all your thoughts and plans, even when you do not see what the Lord is doing.

Do not try to hurry the will of God; difficulty and even disaster can result. I have seen more than one young student make a frantic decision about marriage, only to marry someone who does not have a desire to serve the Lord. Running ahead of God may be as disastrous as not seeking God's will in the first place. Be patient and rest in the certainty that God is in control of all aspects of your life and that the Lord will lead you to the right person and right vocation at the right time.

Remain sensitive to the Spirit's prompting and repent quickly when convicted of wrongdoing or shortcoming. Even when you fall or make mistakes in your walk with God, the Lord keeps guiding you. Your responsibility is to walk in the direction you think God is leading and to ask for assurance or correction. When the Spirit identifies anything you have done that is outside of God's will, quickly repent and ask for cleansing and restoration. Pray the following prayer or one like it: "God, I give you permission to do whatever it takes to keep me from making any more mistakes."

You need not fear such a prayer, if you are convinced that God's will is best for you. If you fear that you will be miserable — asked to go where you do not want to go or do what you do not want to do — you should probably examine your concept of the love of God! If you continue to walk with God in obedience to the Scriptures, then you may trust that your common sense decisions are within God's will unless or until the Spirit convicts you otherwise.

What If You Are Still Unsure?

One of the biggest obstacles to overcome in understanding how God is leading is the tendency to want "instant answers" to everything. Human beings seem predisposed to impatience. Our

society helps condition us to immediacy. Microwave meals, instant foods, and fast technologies spoil us and often create the
attitude that "if it's slow, I don't want it." In this generation more
than any other, perhaps, we cannot begin to fathom the meaning
of "one day is with the Lord as a thousand years, and a thousand
years as one day" (2 Peter 3:8).

"But isn't there anything I can do while I wait for assurance
about how God wants to work through me?" one of my students
asked, after I quoted the verse in 2 Peter to her.

"Walk with God every day, and keep attentive to the situations where the Lord places you," I replied. "Do what God wants
you to do today, and you will be where the Lord wants you
tomorrow."

Learn to serve God here and now. For various reasons, most
of us live today with an eye on the future. When we are children, we can't wait to be teenagers. When we become teens, we
can't wait until we can drive. When we are in high school, we
long for college. When we are in college, we plan for careers and
freedom from our studies. When we are single, we long for marriage. When we get married, we yearn for children. When we
have children, we anticipate their adulthood and our retirement.
On and on goes the saga of living for the future.

This cycle has a problematic influence on our relationship with
God. We often miss opportunities of service and ministry *now*
while we are planning for a future *someday*. A number of years
ago, a young man was killed in an automobile accident during
his last semester of seminary. When I heard about it, I thought,
"How sad to have studied all these years and not get to serve
in the ministry to which God called him." Later I realized that
the young man had only "missed the ministry" if he had failed
to recognize and act on God's call to minister in his present and
not just in his future. *The will of God for the future is the will of
God for now.*

> The Lord has given you a certain set of present circumstances.
> ...Here you must begin; indeed, here you must be willing to re-
> main until other doors of opportunity are perceived and opened.
> The surest way to miss future opportunities is to ignore present

ones.... In the student's calling, there are today's opportunities which God sets before us to prepare us for those of tomorrow. In the lonely student you befriend, the confused roommate you encourage, the article for the college paper that you write, or the Sunday School class you teach may lie the key to your future. It is in the service that you render whether in the classroom or out of it that your gifts are proved and manifested.[3]

Don't demand an answer today. As a teacher, I understand the principle of needing to communicate basic information before asking my students to tackle something more difficult. No one expects a first-grade class to solve mathematical equations when they haven't learned to read the numbers! What is true in academic disciplines is true in spiritual disciplines as well, and like any good teacher, God knows when we are ready to hear a word of direction.

Many Christians are still in spiritual kindergarten class. We must learn certain fundamentals about God's leadership before we can understand more of the particulars. Edmund Clowney draws on a baseball metaphor to explain this principle: "No player is called to a spot on a major league team who had not proved himself in the minors. God's call *to* service normally comes *in* service."[4]

You may long for the time when you know for certain what God has in store for your future, "[b]ut *until then,* your Mission is here in the valley, and the fog, and the little callings moment by moment, day by day. More to the point, it is likely you cannot ever get to your mountaintop Mission unless you have first exercised your stewardship faithfully in the valley."[5]

Focus on service to others. One of the pitfalls of pursuing the will of God for yourself as an individual is the tendency for your vision to become inverted. If you are not careful, your service will become self-centered instead of other-centered. Keep your focus on God and the needs of others in order to escape a destructive self-centeredness. "Take the towel and basin and discover your calling at your brother's feet; go with him to visit the prisoner and find your calling at his side."[6]

Don't sit down and do nothing. Be a good steward of what has been entrusted to you. If you wait until you know for certain in what vocation God will use you, you will probably be at the same place in your quest at this time next year! You are probably aware of some ways God has blessed you already, so look for opportunities to minister. Use your talents in any way you can to serve the Lord and others. Experiment with things you have never tried. Watch for God's working in your life. The Lord is willing to teach when you are willing to learn. God "has already called you — to be a Christian. Fulfill that call with all your heart and you will learn in [God's] time what ministry is yours."[7]

Remember who's in charge of your life. Many people are so afraid of missing God's will that the fear paralyzes them. They become indecisive, fearing that one mistake will destine them to life outside the will of God. If we will be convinced that the Lord wants us to know and do God's will and that the Spirit will take an active role in seeing that we don't make "fatal" mistakes, that assurance will free us to step out along the journey. God knows our weaknesses and has provided us with the indwelling Holy Spirit to be our strength and guide. God knows we need that *inside help!* With the Spirit, you can be assured of God's leadership while you work on your own "follow-ship."

I found posted on the Internet the following poem, written by Rev. Bien A. Llobrera, and it seems to express this confidence clearly:

> To my mind's eye a carpenter appeared,
> Around him lay his tools — a saw, a hammer,
> A measuring rule, and many other tools
> With which he built — perhaps a rich mansion,
> Perhaps a lowly bench — all arranged and ready
> For his use, though he did not use them
> All at the same time. I wondered:
> What if, say, the hammer said, "I'm not
> Being used. I'll go off and help a person
> On my own," what would the master say?
> The Master said to the hammer, "You are
> My servant, a special tool of mine.
> I decided when to use you, where and how
> And why, and for how long I want.

You are not more busy when I take you up;
You are not idle when I put you down.
In or off my hand you are busy, if you're
Constantly yielded to me, ready at any time,
Never leaving your station as a tool
Of mine, nobody else's, mine alone."
And so I looked up to my Master and said,
"Yes, Lord, I am your servant, yours alone,
To live only because you want me to,
Or to die. I am your instrument for building up
Or tearing down, to declare your grace
Or wrath; through me let your wisdom,
Power, and love flow forth, until you have done
What's in your heart and mind. I am
Your servant now and evermore, and I wish for
No other station, no other work, no other life."[8]

Notes

1. Henry Blackaby and Claude King, *Experiencing God* (Nashville: Lifeway Press, 1990), 87.

2. Morris Ashcraft, *The Will of God* (Nashville: Broadman Press, 1980), 22.

3. Edmund P. Clowney, *Called to the Ministry* (Phillipsburg, N.J.: Presbyterian and Reformed Publishing Company, 1964), 37–38.

4. Ibid., 83.

5. Richard N. Bolles, *How to Find Your Mission in Life* (Ten Speed Press, 1991), 38.

6. Clowney, 88.

7. Ibid., 67.

8. Rev. Bien A. Llobrera, First Filipino Baptist Church, Pasadena, California. Reprinted with permission from author.

Chapter Four

EFFECTIVENESS AND
THE CALL TO MINISTRY

In a divinity school class on Religion and Personality, we were examining characteristics of effective ministers. I asked the students to brainstorm the traits they would like to see in a pastor or staff member. We started with the assumption that the ministers were committed Christians.

As the students mentioned specific characteristics, I wrote them on the board so we could see the entire profile. Soon the board was filled with words and phrases describing the "ideal minister." When no one could add anything more to the list, I asked the class to examine the list carefully and to eliminate any quality they thought was not important. No words were erased. Then I asked them to react to the list and to examine their own lives to see which characteristics they did or did not possess. Ironically, although most of the class members were already serving in some ministry position, they admitted that they didn't have all the characteristics they expected of other ministers. In fact, several students confessed that they might need to drop out of school if those were the traits *necessary* for success in the ministry!

Clearly, even candidates for ministry themselves have almost impossible expectations of vocational ministers. As you read this chapter, which deals with traits of effective ministers, keep in mind that there is no such thing as *"The* Effective Minister." Personalities, gifts, and talents are different. Spiritual experiences, call experiences, and theological understandings all differ. Past experiences, families of origin, intellectual capacities, and educational opportunities uniquely influence us and predispose us to be who we are today. Each person has strengths, but we also have weaknesses. Of one thing you can be certain, however: if you are called by God and walk with the Lord on a daily basis in obedience to God's will, the Lord will make you effective in ministry. Don't become discouraged because of the weaknesses you see in your life. Remember, it is in your weakness that God's power is made perfect (2 Corinthians 12:9).

If you are still wondering if the Lord has called you into vocational Christian ministry, consider carefully what others have written about the qualities expected of ministers. God may speak to you through the following descriptions about the areas in your life where the Lord is presently working. Whether or not you ever serve in a ministry vocation, however, this information should be an incentive to grow in maturity. In fact, when my students and I examined our list of characteristics more closely, we discovered them to be traits all Christians should have!

Characteristics of an Effective Minister

According to an Educator

Daniel Aleshire served for many years as a professor of ministerial students, and he now works for the Association of Theological Schools, an agency that accredits seminaries and other theological institutions. He came to three conclusions about essential characteristics that ministers should have.[1] You may be surprised to discover that his emphasis is on "who the minister *is*" instead of only stressing "what the minister *does*."

Authentic and maturing spirituality. Often people take for granted that a minister will be authentic and mature in the area of spirituality, but this quality is not automatic just because a person has entered vocational ministry. Many patterns and habits we develop as students carry over into our working lives. Too often students think they will have more time for Bible study, reflection, prayer, evangelism, and other spiritual disciplines when they aren't so busy with their studies. The truth is, however, that if you have not developed your spiritual disciplines along the journey toward ministry, you will probably not develop them much when the demands of ministry are thrust upon you.

Part of a mature and authentic spirituality is the willingness to explore and accept ways of relating to God that are different from your own; Christian spirituality both respects and grows out of individuality. As a minister, you must be mature enough to allow others to express their spirituality as individuals.

A third aspect of authentic spirituality is self-discipline and a willingness to face your own sinfulness. This does not imply a "morbid preoccupation" with sin, but you should be honest enough to recognize your own fallibility and mature enough to confess it.

An authentic sense of self. Ministry is a "being" profession; in other words, *who* we are determines *how* we are in ministry. You cannot be "angry, broken, and distraught in [your life] and walk into [your job] and be gentle, kind, open, accepting, and caring."[2] Work to develop a healthy identity, knowing who you are, what you like to do, and when you are not being honest with yourself. On the other hand, don't get bogged down in undue introspection, and avoid the pitfall of inverting the "being" equation; your ministry becomes what you are, but you are more than your ministry. People who have an identity based on their jobs are prone to psychological damage when their jobs end or fail.

Some ministers develop a sense of spirituality they think allows them to transcend the bounds of their humanity. Strive to keep a proper perspective on both your humanity and your spirituality. Evidence shows that people who have a positive self-acceptance of their own weaknesses and limitations are more able to be sensitive to others and to forgive themselves and others for past mistakes.

Professional skills. Ministers must acquire the professional skills and knowledge required to be "equippers of the saints." Commitment to the Lord is not enough. You need the right tools and the knowledge to use them, and those tools must be primed for use. You may have the jigsaw in hand, but if you don't know which end of it to use, you will certainly wreak havoc — on yourself and those around you!

Many studies reveal that the pastor is second only to the physician among professionals from whom people seek counseling. Because as much as 80 percent of a pastor's time is spent in some kind of counseling, a minister needs to be trained in identifying serious psychological problems and have the skills necessary to counsel or the discernment to refer when appropriate.

Beyond these observations of Aleshire's, I would assert that, fundamentally, ministry is an expression of discipleship. Only the mature, authentic, and skilled disciple can function effectively as a minister, and these attributes do not happen automatically when the person accepts a ministry position.

Ministers Speak for Themselves

In one study, over five thousand laypersons and clergy from forty-seven denominations were asked to rate 850 descriptions of ministry in order of importance.[3] Out of this study emerged the following characteristics of effective ministry:

1. Having an open, affirming style

2. Caring for persons under stress

3. Evidencing congregational leadership

4. Being a theologian in life and thought

5. Undertaking ministry from a personal commitment of faith

6. Developing fellowship and worship

7. Having denominational awareness

8. Evidencing ministry to community and world

9. Being priestly-sacramental in ministry

10. Manifesting a lack of privatistic, legalistic style

11. Not having disqualifying personal and behavioral characteristics

Bruce Grubbs has been active in ministry assessment for the Southern Baptist Convention, and he reports some interesting findings among ministers who are seeking greater fulfillment in their careers. In their self-assessments, these ministers identified a number of areas crucial to a sense of personal fulfillment in ministry; I have highlighted a few of them here.[4]

Self-acceptance. As suggested by Aleshire, a minister must recognize his or her own strengths and weaknesses. Because many people are tempted to put ministers on pedestals, all too often ministers themselves tend to view themselves unrealistically as well. They "become the role" and lose touch with who they really are outside the profession itself. When they cannot be all things to all people in their ministry, they may develop a sense of worthlessness. Their imperfections can mire them in hypocrisy and despair or exhaust them in perfectionism and burnout.

If you feel called into vocational ministry, you need to understand your personal limitations and learn to accept what can change and what probably will never change.

As a case in point, an introverted friend of mine recently experienced burnout because he had accepted a job designed for an extrovert. Having come to grips with the improbability of success in such a role, he has since accepted a position that suits his personality better. To acknowledge your natural aptitudes and seek to match your strengths to a ministry need is not to exclude the possibility of God acting through your weaknesses, of course. God blesses our availability as much as our abilities, but we have been given common sense to honestly evaluate ourselves and our world.

Personal character and integrity. Although recent years have cast a public shadow on the integrity of certain renowned ministers, most ministers interviewed by Grubbs affirmed the *personal* importance of individual integrity and character. Although as minister you may fool some people all of the time and all people some of the time, *you* have to live with your character or lack thereof every day, and the ministers surveyed by Grubbs agreed that personal fulfillment is impossible without a sense of your own integrity. You may have no one checking on your schedule, your prayer life, your study time, or your inner thoughts and attitudes.

You may be the only one who knows you are not working up to your capacity, but when you are alone with yourself and with God, this matter of personal integrity and character will make or break you in the ministry.

Last year the pastor of a nearby church came to talk with me about a problem in his marriage. During the conversation he used such sordid profanity and evidenced such bitterness that I was shocked. I wondered how he could attempt to preach the holy Word of God on Sunday when his speech during the week was so filthy. Apparently he compartmentalized his life in a way that was harmful to him and his family. He has since divorced his wife and left the ministry.

Are you able to compartmentalize your life into "sacred" and "secular" as that pastor did? Do you fool yourself into thinking that your behavior Monday through Saturday will have no impact on your ministry on Sundays? Think again. Unless you are able to get your life in tune with God and God's holiness, you will be no credit to Christianity, and you should not be in the ministry.

Developing spirituality. The old saying that "familiarity breeds contempt" may be true with persons who deal with spiritual matters on a daily basis. The unique presence of God, the beauties of creation, the power of prayer, the quiet moment of reflection, the depth of the truths of God's Word may all be lost in the routine activities of spirituality a minister must perform every day.

One of the greatest temptations for you as a spiritual leader will be to become so absorbed in the lives of others that you neglect your own walk with God. Constantly giving but never taking time to replenish and refill your own spiritual reservoirs will make you an empty vessel with nothing to give to a thirsty world.

Endurance and patience. You may have heard a church staff member groan, "Every Monday morning I resign." Although this statement is often said in good humor, the fact is many staff members truly feel this way. Why? When Sunday service doesn't go as planned, staff get frustrated; even activities that go well may be so intense that they leave the leadership drained. Church staff regularly face discouragement and disillusionment in their positions as leaders of people who may not want to be led.

In these circumstances, a minister needs to develop patience and endurance. If you become discouraged when you see little fruit of your labors, you may have a tendency to move from church to church looking for the impossible dream. Some research indicates that, although it takes from three to five years just to get to know a congregation and to earn their confidence, in too many churches, pastors and staff stay less than two years.

No matter where your ministry takes you, you must develop patience and endurance if you are to work faithfully in the fields while awaiting any harvest you may be privileged to see.

Attention to personal needs. Many ministers are so busy serving others that they neglect their own needs. When this happens, they are more prone to burnout and depletion. Taking time with the family, time to read and reflect, eliminating negativity, developing a support system, and learning from mistakes are important in this quest for fulfillment in ministry. Develop a hobby and spend time enjoying it; be sure to reserve one day off each week, and take regular vacations. Even more basically, get regular exercise, eat a balanced diet, and maintain a healthy weight. Cardiovascular illnesses are the chief killers of the clergy — and covered dish dinners can kill you! These are just a few of the things that can add to your personal health and happiness as a fulfilled minister of God.

Expectations of the Church

Numerous studies have been done to determine what qualities church members admire in their staff ministers. Although most of these studies have focused on the pastoral ministry, the qualities identified should not be limited to the pastoral minister. The traits described below may be expected of anyone who undertakes vocational Christian ministry. Even though individual churches have distinct personalities and may emphasize different qualities depending on a congregation's own preferences and perceived needs, according to Dennis Campbell, some characteristics are universally admired.[5]

*The church is looking for leaders of deep faith and personal commit-
ment to Jesus Christ,* who are disciplined in their own walks with
God and who can lead congregations into a deeper understanding and relationship with the Lord. Ministers must have an active
prayer life and be students of the Scriptures in pursuit of personal growth and not simply in preparation for sermons or Bible
studies. As a minister, you should never be satisfied with your
spiritual growth; be willing to admit you have not reached perfection. Your church will need you to be someone who worships
God daily, not only when leading services on Sundays.

*The church is looking for leaders who have gifts for intellectual
development and a concern for learning.* While ministers need not
have the same level of academic preparation, they all should continue growing and learning in all areas of their lives. Churches
want their ministers to be knowledgeable about a variety of issues both to their ministries and to the world beyond the church
walls. Your church will want you to be a good teacher, to have
a thorough understanding of the Bible, and to be able to relate
biblical truths to children and youth as well as to adults.

*The church is looking for leaders who have the ability and commit-
ment to apply their learning to the actual work of ordained ministry.*
Congregations want their ministers to come down out of the
"ivory tower," to relate to the real world, and to offer answers for
the problems and struggles people face every day. Church members do want a better understanding of the Bible, but they also
want to know how to apply its principles to daily living. An effective minister will be a skilled communicator, able to speak and
to write effectively. Campbell asserts that most often, laypersons
ask seminary professors to "teach [ministers] to preach."[6]

Your church will want you to have more than the *ability* to
communicate your knowledge in relevant ways. The members
will want you to be *eager* and willing to lead; they will expect
both strength and flexibility from you as their leader. Churches
expect their staff to be visionaries as well as implementers and
facilitators of the vision.

*The church is looking for leaders who have genuine love for people,
outgoing personalities, and developed relational skills.* Many ministers

who fail in these areas become disillusioned with ministry. If you do not love people, you should seriously consider forgoing the pastorate and exploring a ministry where you will not be expected to be an extrovert. There are many areas of ministry that utilize the gifts of people who relate better to ideas and things. If you feel uncomfortable with people, recall that even introverts who derive most of their energy from the world of ideas can learn the relational skills necessary to be successful in ministries that directly relate to people.

Reality Check

Are you wondering how anyone can live up to the expectations of the ministry? The qualifications seem far beyond the reach of *any* one, even those of us who have been in ministry for years. You will have to develop a realistic attitude about these expectations if you are to be successful to any degree in your ministry role. Remember these principles as you consider vocational ministry:

1. *No one* has all the qualities necessary to be the *perfect* minister.

2. If you wait until you think you are *ready* to minister, you'll never get around to it.

3. God does not expect perfection, only willingness.

4. If you were perfect, you wouldn't need God.

5. If you were perfect, you could not identify with your congregation and their problems.

6. God has promised to use you in spite of your limitations.

7. Your ability to admit *your* struggles and imperfections can be an encouragement to your church members in their own difficulties.

8. Growth must be a way of life for you, even (especially) as the minister.

9. God promises to meet your every need when you trust in the Lord.

10. Those whom God calls, God also equips.

For many years, Selection Research, Inc., has helped schools, businesses, and government agencies identify talented candidates for employment. The Nebraska company, which purchased Gallup, Inc., also studied successful leaders in churches. In one study of Catholic priests, they identified certain themes in successful ministry; the responses were organized under the categories of ability, motivation, and work style. As you read these, look for your own strengths you can build upon.[7]

Ability

Presence was defined as "the quality of being regularly and almost spontaneously conscious of God's action in one's life and the lives of others." A minister gifted with this sense of presence is able to help others discern God's presence in their ordinary experiences.

Ministers who are strong **relaters** have "the desire for relationships and a sense of how to build relationships." **Enablers** possess "the ability to assist others' growth." Through their support, teaching, and delegation of tasks, they enable church members to develop their own gifts.

Ministers with a high degree of **empathy** have "a high capacity for using subtle clues to sense others' feelings." They can often sense and articulate another's feelings before that person can.

Courage in a minister is recognized as "the capacity to ask others to make commitments." Ministers who demonstrate this ability can express important ideas without becoming angry and exert authority to delegate when necessary.

Motivation

Ministers with a sense of **mission** have "the ability to perceive the significance in a task that transcends the task itself." Mission-minded ministers help their members discover purpose in their own lives.

Hope characterizes ministers who possess "an optimistic view of the future." When communicated to a congregation, this optimism becomes contagious and helps others begin to visualize a future for the church and for themselves.

Loyalty involves a commitment to the ministerial calling and to the church itself, as a local body and as a denomination with history and tradition. "This identification helps [ministers] through times of crisis in the church." Similarly, ministers who focus on a theme of **community** reveal an "ability to help parishioners interact with one another and feel a sense of belonging."

Ego awareness is characterized as "the ability to identify the events, recognitions, achievements, and feelings that lead to defining oneself as significant." Ministers who are ego-aware are conscious of their own thoughts and feelings, whether positive and negative, and acceptance of those feelings allows those ministers to be more sensitive to others and thus more trustworthy.

Work Style

A minister with **focus** has "the ability to choose a direction and maintain it," to identify goals for him or herself, and to facilitate church members in identifying their own goals. This theme complements the **arranger**, the minister who is proficient in "organizing people, settings, and other elements — for meetings as well as ministry." An arranger is not a dictator who seeks total control, however; the study indicated that this minister is more like a good stage manager.

Another common theme that emerged from the Gallup interviews was dubbed **omni** — "the ability to live with the tension between uncertainty and the desire for wholeness." Omni-ministers are intrigued by and considerate of the unknown, but they are willing to accept ambiguity while encouraging parishioners to further explore the unanswered questions.

Conceptual ministers have "the ability to articulate for [members] the meanings in scripture and in their own experiences" with God. These ministers desire to learn from experience and enable others to do the same.

A minister who is **caring** loves unconditionally and reaches out with sensitivity to those who are under stress. An effective minister is also a **stimulator** who uses engaging communication to engender enthusiasm in the congregation. A sense of **command** in a pastor is the ability to be appropriately assertive and direct without offending others. And on a more practical note, a minister needs to be **business-minded,** able to use criteria for measurement, having definite objectives and an interest in measurable results, and being possessed of entrepreneurial talent.

Self-Evaluation

In addition to the more familiar intelligence and aptitude tests, various objective tests have been devised to give feedback to individuals in the areas of personality, interests, and spirituality. Try to avail yourself of every opportunity to take these tests in order to obtain as much information as you can about yourself. The qualities and characteristics highlighted in this chapter provide a good starting place for self-assessment. Review the previous sections and rank yourself in each area. You might ask someone else whom you trust to "evaluate" you as well; write down your assessments and compare notes. Be realistic about what can and cannot be changed about your own personality traits. Then, on your own or in consultation with a mentor or friend, devise some specific strategies for enhancing your strengths and goals for strengthening your weaknesses. Remember that if you are afraid of honest self-examination, it will be difficult for you to reach your potential in ministry.

Notes

1. Daniel O. Aleshire, "Essentials of a Minister," *Formation for Christian Ministry* (Louisville: Review and Expositor, 1988), 47–59.

2. Ibid., 53.

3. H. Newton Maloney and Laura Majovski, "The Role of Psychological Assessment in Predicting Ministerial Effectiveness," *Review of Religious Research* 28, No. 1 (September, 1986).

4. Bruce Grubbs, "Making Ministry Full," in *Called to Serve, Ministry for the 21st Century,* Joe R. Stacker, compiler (Nashville: Convention Press, 1993), 27–37.

5. Dennis M. Campbell, *Who Will Go for Us?* (Nashville: Abingdon Press, 1994), 32ff.

6. Ibid., 36.

7. Victoria A. Rebeck, "Gifted for Ministry: Setting Up Pastors for Success," *Christian Century* 110 (June 30–July 7, 1993): 670–675.

Chapter Five

WHEN A CALL
IS NOT A CALL

Billy Graham is one of the most well-known ministers of our day — but so is David Koresh.[1] William Carey is best remembered for his mission work on foreign soil — but so is Jim Jones.[2] Bertha Smith served as a missionary to China for many years — but Mary Baker Eddy began her own religion.[3] Both Simon Peter and Judas Iscariot were called to follow Jesus as one of the twelve disciples; both experienced failure in that calling. However, one repented and was restored; the other succumbed to guilt and despair and committed suicide.

All of these people claimed to have heard a call from God to ministry of one kind or another. What made the difference in their experiences? Why are some remembered for their positive contributions while the others are associated with tragedy or false belief? Did they all hear a call from God? What made the difference between one's success and another's failure — the call itself or the individual's response? Is it possible to have a *genuine* call from God to ministry and still wander so far away that we and those who follow us end in ruin? Are we all susceptible to making the same mistakes? Why doesn't God keep us from such terrible errors? Is it better to avoid the call altogether rather than risk the chance of such failure? What can be done to safeguard *our* ministries from ending in disgrace and tragedy?

These and similar questions must be addressed, at least in part, if we are to understand and experience a "healthy" call to ministry and remain genuine in our service for God. The following guidelines and discussion should prove helpful in discerning what

characterizes a valid call from God and a healthy response to
that call.

What Is a Healthy Call Experience?

To gain a clear understanding of what constitutes a healthy call
to ministry, the best place to start is Scripture, looking at some
biblical calls to ministry. Even though these examples involve
people who did not always live up to their calling, Scripture and
Christian tradition attest that these call experiences can be considered healthy ones. From these examples we will draw some
conclusion about healthy calls.

God is the initiator of the call. The Lord called Abram to
leave his country and to go to a land God had chosen. Abram,
later named Abraham, was selected by God to be the patriarch
through whom the Lord would bless all nations. Abram didn't
volunteer for the journey or for the mission of becoming the
"father of the faithful." God called; the man obeyed (Genesis
12:1–4).

Similarly, Moses certainly didn't volunteer to lead the children
of Israel out of Egypt. He even fought the call for a time, but
when he did surrender, he allowed God to use him even when
faced with many difficulties and obstacles (Exodus 3–4).

Isaiah *did* volunteer to serve God, but only after the Lord initiated the encounter and cleansed him. God worked in Isaiah's
life to get him quiet enough to hear, and when God finally spoke,
Isaiah volunteered for service (Isaiah 6:1–8).

The fishermen Peter, James, and John were hard at work when
Jesus called them to discipleship (Matthew 4:18–20). Matthew
was employed at the tax tables when Christ challenged him with
a personal call to service (Matthew 9:9–11). Saul of Tarsus was
working *against* God when he was confronted with the call to
commitment and service and was transformed into Paul, the
great apostle to the Gentiles (Acts 9:1–6). None were seeking
the call to ministry and service, but all were obedient when the
call came.

God makes clear what the individual must do immediately, although the future may remain veiled. Abram knew he had to leave his country, but he didn't know where he was going. Moses understood he was to go speak to Pharaoh, but he had no way of knowing what the next forty years would bring. When Jeremiah responded to the call to become a faithful spokesman for God, he certainly didn't realize he would wind up in the bottom of a cistern (Jeremiah 38:1–6)! The disciples were asked to follow Jesus, but they did not know what that commitment would entail. Paul knew God wanted him to be an apostle of Jesus, but he did not anticipate how much he would have to suffer for Christ's name.

God's call confronts the individual with a decision, and often the decision is resisted. Moses tried to reason his way out of the call by saying he couldn't speak well. Jonah knew what God wanted him to do, but he didn't want to do it (Jonah 1:1–3). Some people, like Jeremiah and Timothy, felt they were too young (Jeremiah 1:4–10; 1 Timothy 4:11–16). Some, like Jonah and Paul, had to be severely dealt with before they would heed the call God issued. But each individual knew God had spoken, and each had to make a decision whether to be obedient to the call.

God's call should leave the individual feeling humble, not proud. When individuals saw the holiness of the God who was calling them, they realized their own unworthiness. Moses and Jeremiah felt unworthy to speak the holy words of God. Isaiah recognized his own sinfulness and the sinfulness of those among whom he lived (Isaiah 6:5). Paul considered himself the "chief sinner" (1 Timothy 1:15). Thus, if you feel superior to others or have the attitude that "God really picked a good one in me," that arrogance may indicate your response is an unhealthy one. Christ has called us to be servants among the people, not lords over them (Matthew 20:25–28; 1 Peter 5:2–3). When God speaks to you, you will recognize God's worth, your own sinfulness, and the Spirit's grace.

God calls us to relationship as well as to duty. Jesus, himself, was called to full-time ministry, but he also took time to get away and talk with his heavenly Father (Luke 15:16). Even when threatened with death, the prophet Daniel continued to pray and give thanks to God (Daniel 6:10). Moses shouldered many responsibilities and faced many trials as he attempted to lead God's people, yet he still set aside time and space to worship and sing praises to God (Exodus 15). Your primary concern as a person who has experienced a call to ministry should be to maintain a vital relationship with the One who has called you. If your call experience in any way draws you away from this vital relationship and dependency, yours is not a healthy response. To love the gift more than the Giver is to err. If you rejoice in the call more than in the Caller, something is very wrong.

God's call is open for examination by oneself and by others. Jeremiah had doubts about his calling, but he shared his fears with God (Jeremiah 1:6–8). Samuel was willing to receive instruction from Eli (1 Samuel 3:1–10). Barnabas helped both Paul and John Mark to mature in their understanding and ministries (Acts 9:27; 15:37–39). If you are reluctant to discuss your call experience with others, especially with those who understand the calling to ministry, your reluctance may indicate a problem. In my studies of those who have begun cult groups, I discovered many had their call experiences when they were in their teens. Perhaps if these cult leaders had sought the counsel of more mature Christians, who could have helped them evaluate their experiences, then the world might have been spared the pain of so many false religious groups.

God's call often comes when an individual is already involved in the Lord's service. Isaiah and Jeremiah were already active in temple ministry when their prophetic calls were issued (Isaiah 6; Jeremiah 1). Elisha was something of an understudy of Elijah until he received his own commission to minister (1 Kings 19:19–20; 2 Kings 2:9–11). Many people testify that their calls to ministry grew out of their ministry as lay leaders in the church. When you are faithful in the tasks that God has already given to you, the Lord may reveal to you a calling to serve in other ways, perhaps in full-time or bi-vocational ministry.

Many of God's calls come in the recognition of others' needs. Habakkuk's call to prophetic ministry came as he struggled with the issue of the prosperity of the wicked (Habakkuk 1). When Isaiah took his first look at people around him, he was overwhelmed with their sinfulness and his own. But after he was cleansed and began to listen to the voice of God, his second look caused him to volunteer to reach others (Isaiah 6:8–9). When God fills you with the Spirit's love and compassion, you too may hear the Lord saying, "Will you go for me?"

Many people feel a call to missions as they hear missionaries speak of the overwhelming needs in other parts of the world. Many young people feel the first tug of a call to ministry as they visit nursing homes or homeless shelters or participate in mission trips with their church groups. Perhaps more people would answer God's call if churches would provide more opportunities for their congregations to see that the "fields are white for harvest" (John 4:35).

God often uses others to challenge an individual to answer the call and to follow it more faithfully. The Lord used Mordecai to exhort Esther to respond to God's calling (Esther 4:12–14). The prophet Nathan challenged David when the king failed to act rightly in his calling (2 Samuel 12:1–10). God used Barnabas in the lives of Paul and John Mark to help them follow Christ's leading (Acts 9:26–27; 15:36–40), and in turn, Paul was used in the lives of Timothy and Titus, two preacher boys (Acts 16:1–5; Galatians 2:1–3). The Lord often uses pastors, youth ministers, parents, and teachers to help young people understand and follow the path of God's leading.

When God issues a call, the Lord also provides the resources and opportunities necessary for the call to bear fruit. God provided Aaron as a mouthpiece for Moses (Exodus 4:10–15). Gideon was given the human resources and the battle plan to defeat the Midianites (Judges 7). Jeremiah was touched by God and given the words he needed to prophesy (Jeremiah 1:9–10). I have seen the heartbreak of Christians who have obtained their educations only to find the door of service closed to them. Some were unable to find churches or other places of ministry. Some applied for missions, only to be rejected by their mission boards. I have to conclude one of the following reasons for the difficulties:

(1) they misunderstood the call of God for their lives, (2) they are unwilling to go where the Lord wants them to go, and/or (3) they are still on the pathway and should be faithful in service while they wait for the doors to open. When God calls, with the call comes the assurance that the Lord will provide the place of service and the resources to accomplish God's purpose.

God's call will match the talents and gifts of the individual called. The apostle Paul's commitment to and zeal for religion vitalized his determination to reach the world for Christ (Galatians 1:13–24). Timothy's nurture in a Christian home was a solid foundation on which to build his ministry of nurturing others in the house of faith (2 Timothy 1:5). Peter's former career as a fisherman became the metaphor for his ministry, when Jesus called him to become a "fisher of men" (Mark 1:16–17). God has created us and given us certain abilities; the Lord will use those abilities in service in various places in ministry. Nothing is sadder than seeing young people attempt to go into ministry vocations for which they are not gifted. As mature Christians, we should show our love to these young people by affirming the strengths we do see in them rather than standing by and watching them stumble toward disaster.

What Is an Unhealthy Call Experience?

Although we may want to deny it, the evidence indicates that unhealthy call experiences exist along with the healthy ones. One of the biggest obstacles to overcome in looking at this issue is our own subjectivity. We all want to think our own experiences of the call to ministry are healthy, and you may be uneasy about thinking otherwise. As you read this portion of the book and consider what experience has taught *me*, ask God for wisdom to see your weaknesses as well as your strengths, the toxic portions of your call and faith as well as the healthy parts. Remember: the Great Physician can heal any illness we have.

Some unhealthy call experiences originate with an external source, often arising from well-meaning but overzealous counsel. Unfortunately some people are so eager to recruit workers for the harvest that they do the recruiting themselves. A church and its minister are blessed to have someone in the congregation answer God's call to ministry, but the church is not to do the calling. Of course, when ministers are faithful to teach and preach God's Word to their congregations, people will grow in their faith, and they may be more open to respond to God's call. However, that call is God's own, initiated by the Spirit and not by anything human beings do. Pray that the Lord of the harvest thrust forth laborers into the fields. And if those laborers are members of your church, rejoice! If they are not, rejoice all the same!

One special word of caution to church staff: be sure to make no assumptions but to counsel your young people in the correct way. Many of my students who have responded to God's call to some form of ministry tell me that, when they made their decision public in the church, their pastors interpreted their call before the whole church as a call to preach. And that wasn't what these students had said at all! After such a statement has been made, however, when these young people follow God's leading into a different ministry, church members wonder why they are "settling for less." (That sense of "settling for less" may imply that preaching is valued above any other vocation or simply the misunderstanding that if the young person was called to one ministry, pursuing any other vocation is missing out on God's best.)

Family members or spouses may also be the source of unhealthy call experiences. Family members who are in the ministry themselves may desire to "carry on the family heritage." Others are godly parents or grandparents who have dedicated their children to God and who think the most wonderful way God could use these children is in vocational ministry. Family can influence in direct and indirect ways and try to push a loved one in the direction of ministry without seeking God's will for that individual through prayer and study of the Scriptures.

Similarly, some spouses push their mates in the direction of ministry because they feel led in that direction themselves. If your spouse feels called into ministry, he or she should ask God to issue the same call to you. In turn, you should share your own feelings and talk with your mate, asking him or her to pray about God's call for your marriage and your family. Sometimes you will need to wait and pray until God makes the calling clear to both of you.

Some unhealthy call experiences originate from an internal source. In case you have not already noticed, we are very complicated people! Forces within us affect us in ways of which we are utterly unconscious. Before looking at some of these "unconscious" influences and how they affect our call responses, however, consider some familiar, "nonspiritual" gut reactions.

Have you ever heard a song and suddenly felt a strong sense of sadness because of a memory associated with it? Have you ever been hurt or offended someone and discovered that the same emotions surface when you meet someone who has the same name? Have you ever watched a scary movie and found yourself terrified later when you are alone or in a similar place? Have you felt romantic after you hear a song that was played years ago at your senior prom or at your wedding? Have you had anger well up in your heart when you hear the echo of words that remind you of how someone mistreated you in the past?

Even these innocuous examples reveal how past experiences can affect our present thoughts and feelings in powerful ways. Imagine how much more we are influenced by more traumatic experiences, such as a family history of abuse, divorce, or alcoholism or a personal history of broken relationship, tragic loss, or violent crime. Even if your history is not so "dramatic," you can never be fully aware of how past experiences influence your present. Be on the lookout for its effects; they are surely there!

Consider the themes highlighted below and evaluate for yourself how these powerful emotions and needs might surface in your life and influence your response to God's call to service and ministry.

Guilt and Shame

Some people go into the ministry driven by a guilty conscience. I have noticed this especially in Christians who, having accepted

Jesus as Savior at an early age, drifted into a wicked and rebellious lifestyle. When these individuals repent and return to the
Lord, many of them are unable to forgive themselves. They experience tremendous guilt over their sinful past because they were
professing Christians at the time of their moral rebellion. When
they do come back to God, they experience what they interpret
as a call to preach — but which may be more of a misplaced zeal
that carries their recommitment to the opposite extreme.

Let me hasten to add that not all people who are called out of
a sinful lifestyle or a backslidden condition experience unhealthy
calls. There are exceptions to this and all of the examples I give.
All the same, I urge you to examine your own motives and your
own call to the ministry. If you are called out of a sense of guilt,
out of a desire to "pay God back" for forgiving you, that "call" is
an unhealthy one that will cause you great difficulty in the future
if you don't come to terms with it.

On the other hand, if you have begun with an unhealthy response, that does not negate the possibility that God may still
want you to be in vocational Christian ministry. But first, you will
need to understand and change some areas of your life before the
ministry to which you are called can be a fruitful one.

A Need for Power or Control

Anyone who has been a church member for very many years is
aware that some people seem to thrive in the midst of a power
struggle. A pastor leaves, the new pastor arrives, and in many
churches a power struggle begins as people try to get on the best
side of the new minister. At the same time, the new minister is
usually busy trying to figure out the power structures among the
people!

Inevitably, during business meetings or committee meetings,
some self-appointed boss wants to have the last say in a decision.
I have observed that the people who cause the most trouble with
their need to control are the ones whose lives are out of control in some way. Some of them work in jobs where they have
little or no say in what is going on. Others come from families
where they felt their lives were out of control. Out of unstable

family systems or disempowered work environments, people experience a need to save the world by exerting control over it. Some interpret this need as a call to ministry, the ultimate way to save wayward individuals. And as they follow this unhealthy call, their own need to be in control of people and outcomes drives them to be controlling preachers, dictatorial Christian education directors, or workaholic worship leaders. They desperately try to fix the world in order to find the peace and stability they could never find in their own out-of-control lives. When they encounter difficulties, they try even harder and become even more controlling.

The infamous cult leader Rev. Jim Jones exhibited various tendencies that suggest to me that he came from a dysfunctional family background, not the least of which characteristics were his tendency toward paranoia, thinking everyone was out to destroy him, and his need to be in complete control of his "flock" at all times. His failure to control and rescue others from what he deemed to be the ills of society led him to take his followers to Guyana; there he rescued them in the only way he had left — mass suicide.

A Need for Prestige or Recognition

All of us need to feel a sense of worth, in ourselves and in relation to others. Recently I visited the home of a physician and his family. He is a prominent doctor in our area, and although the family does not need a second income, his wife has chosen to work part-time for an agency that is striving to prevent child abuse in our county. This woman goes into schools and communities to teach children ways of keeping themselves safe from abuse. I have never asked her why she takes her time to do this, but I am certain I already know part of the reason. Her work makes her life seem more worthwhile.

I heard the same answer last summer from a man I met while on vacation in the Golden Isles in Georgia. He drove the sightseeing trolley I rode to tour the island. While talking with him during one of our stopover breaks, I learned that he had made a million dollars as a thirty-year-old and had retired a few years before at the ripe old age of forty! He told me that, although he has more money than he knows how to spend, he needed something to do to make his life seem worthwhile. So, he bought the trolley and spends his days showing tourists around the island.

Everyone needs something to do that makes life seem worthwhile, but while this is a noble motivation for many things — like working after retirement or doing part-time or volunteer work for a good cause — seeking a sense of self-worth should not be the reason you enter a vocational Christian ministry. If you are driven into ministry or missions out of the need to feel good about yourself, you are setting yourself up for discouragement and failure when the people you serve don't respond with the affirmation and appreciation you crave.

Self-Evaluation

Do you observe some unhealthy characteristics in your own call experience? If so, don't panic. We all have areas where we need to grow and improve. No one has "arrived." We all need to work at improving ourselves mentally, emotionally, physically, and spiritually.

Try to look at your strengths and weaknesses without feeling self-conscious about doing so. Examine your past and how it has affected you, but do not wallow in undue anger or shame because of negative experiences. Because you need a foundation that can withstand questions and examination without threatening you, take time to write down what you *do* believe about life, spiritual truths, values, and so forth, and examine why you have affirmed those beliefs. Be open to those who disagree with you; they may be able to share insight that will help you grow.

If you discover that some of your service to others has been motivated by unhealthiness in your life or past experiences, know that God's grace is sufficient to transform you into the healthy servant the Lord wants you to be. God may or may not be calling you to vocational Christian ministry, but you can be assured that God *is* calling you to be the best Christian you can possibly be. With that goal in mind, be open and willing to change when the Spirit shows you areas of weakness, even if the Lord uses someone else to point them out to you!

Notes

1. Known for his Branch Davidian cult in Waco, Texas, where he died in a fiery explosion while resisting arrest.

2. Known for taking his congregation to Guyana and leading them in a mass suicide.

3. Credited with founding the Christian Science religion.

Chapter Six

ACKNOWLEDGING AND
ACCEPTING A CALL

Neither my friend, Dennis Hester, nor his family attended church when he was a child. He quit school when he was in the tenth grade, having failed the first and fifth grades. He became a Christian at age nineteen and began attending a small Baptist church in a tiny town in North Carolina where he was active in the church's youth group. He participated in ministry as opportunities for serving were presented. The church family affirmed him in his efforts, especially when he preached. His goal in life, however, was to become a country music star.

> It would often make me angry when someone would say to me after I had preached a sermon, "Have you ever thought about entering the ministry?" or "I believe God is calling you to preach." I was angry because I knew God was calling me to return to school and prepare for the ministry. I had hated school and had so many bad memories, I couldn't bear the thought of returning to school.

He wondered how he could possibly preach when he felt so insecure and uneducated. He "chased every rainbow," working at numerous jobs but finding no satisfaction in any of them. Every time he attended church, he came under heavy conviction from the Lord. One evening, in his bedroom, he stared out the window and in desperation prayed to God, "Lord, I have tried every kind of job I can think of. I have searched every dream, but nothing has satisfied me. I have been running from you. I feel so inadequate. But I feel you want me to preach. So, if preaching is what you want me to do, I will do the very best that I can."

From that night on, he had an unexplainable sense of peace and security. Dennis Hester would return to school and become a pastor, an author, and a minister of the gospel of Jesus.

Running from God's Call

I have worked for more than twenty years with students in college and divinity school. Many of them have shared with me how they ran from God's call to ministry before finally surrendering. Since this was not my experience when God called me, I was interested to learn why so many people have felt — and still feel — the need to run from God's call. My study began with the most widely known biblical story of someone who fled from the call of God: Jonah. Although the story does not answer as many questions as it raises, perhaps it does provide some very helpful insights about why some people run from God and the consequences of doing so.

First, when God speaks, *the Spirit makes clear what the Lord wants for that specific moment in time.* Since the Spirit usually gives very few details and rarely forecasts the outcome of our obedience to God's call, some people are reluctant to obey when the call first comes. If that is the case with you, try to remember that God will give you enough direction to take the next step. Concentrate on being obedient to what you do know is God's will while waiting for the Lord to reveal the rest.

> The word of the Lord came to Jonah son of Amittai: "Go to the great city of Nineveh and preach against it, because its wickedness has come up before me." (Jonah 1:1–2)

We are not told *how* God made this call clear to Jonah or what Jonah was doing, where he was, or what his previous experiences with God had been. We only know that God spoke and Jonah apparently understood what God told him.

We might speculate that the difficulty with Jonah was low self-esteem, the feeling that he was not up to the task of preaching in such a large city. We may guess that the wickedness of the great city or his own prejudices against it sent him sailing off in the opposite direction. No one knows exactly why Jonah resisted God's call, but the questions raised by this story should help you reflect on your own experiences.

Are you running from the task God has called you to accomplish? Why? Are you insecure and uncertain, struggling with low self-esteem? Have you forgotten God's promise to be with you always (Matthew 28:19–20; Hebrews 13:5)? Has God placed on your heart a work to do that you are not willing to do? Are you shrinking back from going somewhere or ministering to people you don't like? What other reasons do you give for resisting God's call?

Second, if God calls us to a special task, *the Lord will continue to work with us even when we run in the opposite direction.* Whenever we run from the call of God, in essence we are running from God's presence. We may disguise or deny this reality in many ways, but our relationship with God is hindered when we are disobedient concerning the Lord's call.

> But Jonah ran away from the Lord and headed for Tarshish. He went down to Joppa, where he found a ship bound for that port. After paying the fare, he went aboard and sailed for Tarshish to flee from the Lord. (Jonah 1:3)

If you are running from God's call, you probably aren't so bold that you physically run in the opposite direction as Jonah did, but you can flee from God's call in other ways. Are you staying busy to avoid thinking about what God is saying to you? Are you trying to escape by "doing good" but still missing out on "God's best"? Have you even left the church and spiritual things and embarked upon a sinful lifestyle? Or you do mask your disobedience by saying you aren't sure what God wants? Whatever you do to avoid answering the call of God will not prevent the Lord from working with you. Hopefully, you will not be so disobedient that God has to use drastic means to get your attention!

Third, *our own disobedience can cause difficulties in the lives of others we encounter.* Often when we are disobedient to God's will for us, people around us suffer.

> Then the Lord sent a great wind on the sea, and such a violent storm arose that the ship threatened to break up.... So they asked him, "Tell us, who is responsible for making all this trouble for us? What do you do?" (Jonah 1:4, 8)

We do not live in isolation. Friends and family members feel the effects of our disobedience to God. Many a life has been shipwrecked or a ministry ruined because of the disobedience of someone who is running from the call to ministry.

Sometimes family or friends become an excuse for not following God. Do you reason that your obedience will adversely affect your family? Do you hesitate to leave your secure job to go back to school? Do you rationalize that your family could not adjust to a move to another state, much less to another country? Are you avoiding the call by trying to convince yourself that *you* are responsible for the happiness and well-being of your family members; therefore, God could not possibly be calling you to do *that* or to go *there?* Remember that your responsibility is to be obedient to God's leadership. The Lord will take care of all of your needs (Philippians 4:19) as well as those of your family. Your family will be much better off in Nineveh if you are in the center of God's will than they would be if you dragged them with you on a storm-tossed ship going to Tarshish!

Fourth, *when we run away, our first move back into the center of God's will is to admit and confess where we went astray.* The first step for Jonah was admission that he was the cause of the difficulties his shipmates were experiencing.

> The sea was getting rougher and rougher. So they asked him, "What should we do to you to make the sea calm down for us?" "Pick me up and throw me into the sea," he replied, "and it will become calm. I know that it is my fault that this great storm has come upon you." (Jonah 1:11–12)

Often the Lord has to allow us and those around us to become miserable before we will submit and willingly follow God's lead. Many people who have run from God, only to surrender to the Spirit's call later, testify to how unhappy they were until they surrendered. What a joy it would be for us to develop a "yes, sir" attitude toward Christ, our Captain. To hear God speak and to immediately answer, "Yes, Lord. I'd be happy to!" — that is the goal.

Are you running from God's will for your life? Maybe you have begun to realize that you will never experience complete peace until you surrender. You know deep in your heart what God has been trying to tell you for some time. Perhaps you are established in a good career and own your own home. You and your family may be happy in your community and active in your local church. But deep down inside, when you shut out the clamor of the world's activities and listen to the Spirit's still, small voice, you know that Christ has called you. You are moving toward the place of being willing to say, "Yes, sir."

Fifth, *sometimes God has to make the storm severe and isolate us from others* before we are quiet enough to hear and desperate enough to surrender.

> Then they took Jonah and threw him overboard, and the raging sea grew calm.... But the Lord provided a great fish to swallow Jonah, and Jonah was inside the fish three days and three nights.... From inside the fish Jonah prayed to the Lord his God. (Jonah 1:15, 17; 2:1)

Desperate disobedience often makes parents resort to desperate methods to reach a disobedient child. Only as Jonah prayed and reflected from the belly of that great fish was God able to bring him to the place where he was willing to do what God had been trying to get him to do. Have you been running so long and hard from God's call on your life that the Lord must use desperate means to reach you? What storm in your life might be God's way of getting your attention? What "great fish" might God use to carry you to the depths of the silence of your own heart?

Sixth, *difficulties in life often are the events that cause us to become willing to do God's will.* After nearly drowning and spending three days inside a big fish, when God called the second time, Jonah agreed to go to Nineveh with a hearty, "Yes, Lord!"

> Then the word of the Lord came to Jonah a second time: "Go to the great city of Nineveh and proclaim to it the message I give you." Jonah obeyed the word of the Lord and went to Nineveh. (Jonah 3:1–3)

God worked with Jonah until Jonah was ready to follow, even when it meant going to a city he despised and preaching to a people he didn't like. Even then, Jonah's lessons in obedience were only beginning.

Perhaps you are at a similar place in your commitment to God's call on your life. Perhaps you have taken the first steps of obedience; perhaps you have sold your home, given up your job, or started your academic training. You may even be exercising your spiritual gifts of ministry. These are certainly steps in the right direction, but there are more lessons ahead — a lifetime of them, in fact!

Finally, *we must learn how to obey God's call but leave the results up to the Lord.* Many of us try to figure out how God will work out our ministry. Then, when life takes a direction different from the one we had imagined, we become discouraged or angry.

> On the first day, Jonah started into the city. He proclaimed: "Forty more days and Nineveh will be overturned...." When God saw what [Nineveh] did and how they turned from their evil ways, he had compassion and did not bring upon them the destruction he had threatened. But Jonah was greatly displeased and became angry. (Jonah 3:4, 10; 4:1)

Jonah had much more to learn — and so do we. Jonah's mistakes were obvious; we can learn from them. *First,* he was more concerned about the success of his ministry than he was about the lives of those to whom he ministered. *Second,* his understanding of the love and compassion of God was obviously lacking. *Third,* he continued to justify his initial unwillingness to answer God's call, using this change of events as rationalization for running in the opposite direction.

> O Lord, is this not what I said when I was still at home? That is why I was so quick to flee to Tarshish. (Jonah 4:2)

Have you encountered problems or experienced failure after you started on your journey of obedience to God's call? Are you indulging in self-pity or depression because the road has taken a turn you did not anticipate? Have you been questioning whether you made a mistake following God at all? Be assured that God will continue to work in your life. The Lord will renew your vision for a world of hurting people who need to hear the message of God's love. The Lord may allow you to have your "pity party," but at some point God will provide some worms to eat the excuses you are using. Peace and joy will return when you again see the world through God's eyes and when you join with God in ministering to it.

Why Others Ran from God's Call

In a survey I conducted as part of the research for this book, I asked respondents some questions about the reasons why some people run from God's call. Three hundred sixty-five people from twenty-eight different denominations replied, so I think the information is reliable. Subsequently I discovered that a similar survey had been conducted in 1949 by Ralph Felton.[1] I compared his survey results with mine, and the similarity in the answers made me consider that call experiences have not changed much throughout history.

The respondents to my survey indicated it took an average of *three years* from the time they sensed a call to ministry to the time they accepted the call. Only 13 percent of the respondents said they answered the call immediately, when they first sensed it.

You may wonder, as I did, what caused the majority of individuals to run from or be confused about God's call. The results from Felton's survey and my own give us some insight.

At this point in our investigation, it may be helpful to examine each of these "obstacles" and consider ways to overcome them. Clearly, your willingness to take an honest look at your own life is the first step to overcoming any obstacles that may stand in the way of responding to God's call on *your* life.

Factors that interfered with the call decision

1949 Felton Survey	*1995 Cullinan Survey*
1. Lack of Bible knowledge and feeling of unworthiness	1. Feeling of unworthiness
2. Lack of counseling or guidance	2. Fear of the unknown
3. Financial obligations	3. Other (including, parental objections, spouse's concerns, educational requirements, etc.)
4. Lack of knowledge about ministry	4. Financial obligations

Lack of Bible Knowledge / Feeling of Unworthiness

Some of the other answers given by the survey respondents actually shed some light on why this "excuse" was listed at the top both in 1949 and 1995. In 1949, 68 percent of those surveyed indicated that they had submitted to God's call by age twenty-one; that percentage had dropped only to 60 percent in the 1995 survey. Not surprisingly, a typical twenty-one-year-old does not feel adequate to be a minister!

Someone might feel a sense of unworthiness in answering a call to ministry for a variety of reasons, however. Typically, young adults have an idealized image of those who are our ministers. Individuals fresh out of high school or college do not often see the struggles, weaknesses, and personal feelings of unworthiness with which their pastors and mentors wrestle. As a layperson, especially as a young layperson, you may assume that your clergy and other spiritual leaders have reached a state of spiritual and emotional wholeness that seems foreign to your own experience. Consequently, when you sense God is calling you to serve as a minister, you do not see how you could ever live up to that perceived standard.

You can begin to overcome this obstacle in several ways, but first make sure you are not just making excuses to avoid the calling. To guard against such excuse-making, do an "honesty check" by asking yourself some tough questions — and answer them honestly! Are you willing to consider a call to ministry or missions? What, specifically, do you perceive as obstacles to accepting that call? Can you overcome those obstacles and weaknesses with God's help and real effort on your part? If so, are you willing to make that effort and accept God's help? Are you willing to make the necessary sacrifices? If you truly do struggle with a sense of unworthiness, some of the following activities may be helpful.

Talk with those who are in the ministry. You may discover that a sense of inadequacy for the task is common, even among those serving in the role. Ask them to share with you their own fears about answering God's call for themselves. Ask them how they deal with feelings of inferiority and low self-esteem.

Identify the specific areas where you feel inadequate, and develop a strategy for strengthening those weaknesses. Start with the areas you can improve upon now, but realize much of the equipping for ministry will come as you continue your education. Get involved in some ministry that will challenge you to grow. Each time you serve in some ministry, the task will become easier for you.

Try to discover why you have a negative self-image, and then work against it. Low self-esteem can hamper you in any vocation. Don't be afraid to let others help you develop in areas where you need assistance. Ask more mature Christians who know you well what strengths they see in you. Write a list of your strengths and what you can do to make them even stronger; then write a list of your weaknesses and what you can do to overcome them. Work on overcoming your weaknesses and enhancing your strengths. Do this in a systematic way.

Identify the talents and abilities with which God has gifted you and strengthen them. As you have positive experiences in ministry activities in your church, you will become more confident in how God can use you in Christian service. If you do not know your spiritual gifts, read some books on the subject. Take some interest inventories at school. Ask others what talents they see in you.

If you feel inadequate in your Bible knowledge or education, begin a systematic way to study and learn. Consult your church staff and other Christians you admire to get their suggestions on how you can learn more about the Bible. And be sure to keep in mind that much of your training for ministry will take the form of university and seminary studies.

Lack of Counsel and Guidance / Fear of the Unknown

Most of us fear what we do not understand. Many times our worst enemy is our own ignorance. If we would only take time to discover the facts about a situation, we would fear it no longer.

Have you ever asked someone else what his or her call experience was like? Do you know what is expected of a pastor or other minister? Talking with people who are in the kinds of ministry to which you feel drawn will be extremely beneficial as you seek to understand God's will for your life.

In the two surveys, the respondents were asked to identify the people who were most influential in helping them understand and submit to the call of God. In both surveys, the top-rated person was the respondent's pastor. These "seekers after truth" overcame their fears, at least in part, by asking for guidance from their pastors. You may want to do the same thing. Talk with your pastor or other church staff person. Find out all you can about the pastorate, missions, and other avenues of ministry.

Perhaps more confusion surrounds missions than any other ministry opportunity. The old stereotype of the missionary — living in a grass hut, single and lonely, eating grasshoppers and keeping watch for stray tigers — is far from the truth! But these kinds of misconceptions cause some people to be afraid when they sense God's call to such a ministry.

Financial Obligations

Another issue that surfaced on the two surveys was a concern about financial matters. Especially for the respondents who held an established job, owned a house, and had started a family, these financial concerns seemed legitimate. They asked themselves,

"How can I give up all of this to return to school?" or "Why can't I just serve God where I am in the job I now have?"

Study of the Scriptures provides prompt answers to these and similar questions regarding finances. Reflect upon the following texts:

> And my God will meet all your needs according to his glorious riches in Christ Jesus. (Philippians 4:19)

> But seek first his kingdom and his righteousness, and all these things will be given to you as well. (Matthew 6:33)

> Anyone who loves his father or mother more than me is not worthy of me; anyone who loves his son or daughter more than me is not worthy of me; and anyone who does not take his cross and follow me is not worthy of me. (Matthew 10:37–38)

Through many years of counseling students, I have learned that they worry about finances even before they have any obligations! All of us seem to crave financial security, even when we are just speculating about the future. "I want to be able to provide for my family," says one who doesn't have a family yet. Another comments, "I don't do well at this 'faith thing' of trusting God for each dollar."

These nebulous future concerns are valid, but we need to remember at least one basic truth: God recognizes our financial needs and expects us to plan for them. Our mistake comes in thinking that provision cannot be made within a ministry vocation. While financial security should not be our major concern, financial responsibility certainly is important. God expects us to be hard workers, not beggars. We can rest assured that God will be faithful to the promise to provide for us.

Talk with people who are in ministry about your financial concerns. Learn to be financially responsible *now* with whatever resources God has given to you at this point in your life. Even if you are still dependent on your parents, be responsible with the money they entrust to you and with whatever income you might earn yourself. Scripture tells us that, as we are faithful with what resources we do have, God often entrusts us with more (Matthew 28:13).

Lack of Knowledge about Ministry

Each semester our school invites prospective students to come to campus for a tour and a conference with professors. Each department provides a "booth" at which prospective students and parents can find information about the majors within that department. Representative faculty are present to answer specific questions.

One of the questions most often raised by parents visiting my booth is "How can my child make a living with a religion major?" Their concern, while valid, usually reveals a lack of awareness about vocational opportunities within the field of Christian ministry. Such a lack of knowledge may be one of the reasons some people run from answering God's call to ministry. They cannot envision themselves as a preacher or foreign missionary, so they run from the call altogether. Perhaps that has been a problem for you.

Scattered throughout this book are suggestions for how to discover the diverse ministry opportunities available to you. But remember, many of the actual "specifics" about your vocation may come after you respond to God's initial call. Usually, the Lord desires your willingness to go before the Spirit reveals more information about your destination. Just imagine how it would have been if Abram had refused to leave his homeland until God had told him exactly where he was going!

A Look Within

Take a few moments now and reflect on the following questions. Prayerfully consider where you are at this point in your life regarding God's call. Remember to be obedient to what you do know and commit what you do not know yet to God's timing. The will of God is not a blueprint but an invitation to walk day by day with the Lord Jesus, himself. Specifics will come later. Obedience is what God wants today.

Have you identified some ways in which you may be trying to run from the Lord's call for your life? Have you examined how your obedience or disobedience to the Lord's call may affect others in your family? Have you identified some "storms" and other external events the Lord is using or has used to speak to you? Have you asked the Lord to speak to you through circumstances in your life, and are you willing to follow where God leads?

Are you willing to follow the Lord even if you do not understand fully what that commitment means or where the journey will take you? Have you developed a "yes, Lord" attitude and a willingness to do whatever the Lord wants you to do? Are you willing to leave the results of your ministry in the Lord's hands, even if they are different from what you have hoped they will be?

Note

1. Ralph A. Felton, *New Ministers* (Madison, N.J.: Drew Theological Seminary, 1949).

Chapter Seven

WHAT MINISTRY OPPORTUNITIES ARE AVAILABLE?

One of the major concerns a person has after answering a call to ministry is trying to understand what that means about a specific vocation. Traditionally, any call to ministry has been interpreted to be a call either to the pastorate or to the mission field. When a female expressed a sense of calling, people usually assumed that she would become a nurse and go to Africa! Not so any more. God is calling young and old, male and female, to serve in many different ways and in many different places.

This chapter will consider some of the many ways a person can serve the Lord in "full-time" ministry. One word of caution is worth repeating: your daily walk with God is more important than knowing all of the specifics about a call to serve. However, at some point in the journey, you will have to make a decision regarding a specific vocation. The Lord may use the following information as well as your own experiences to clarify some of the particulars about ministry.

Gathering Helpful Information

When you answer God's call to ministry, one of the first things you should do is start a file on possible ministry vocations. A good place to begin is with your pastor and other church staff members. In your file, include the following for each potential vocation:

- The ministry position.

- Major responsibilities and sample job descriptions.

- Qualifications required (e.g., education, practical experience).

- Interview results. Ask pastors, missionaries, and others in ministry about the advantages and disadvantages of their positions, and keep notes from the discussions.

- Journal information regarding any experiences you have in this type of ministry role (e.g., internships, mission trips, camp experiences where you participated or exercised leadership, books on the subject, etc.).

Talk to as many people as you can about different ministry opportunities. School guidance counselors, college and seminary professors, and people who are on the front line of ministry service are usually very willing to help others who are exploring God's call on their lives. Research the library for books on ministry vocations. Most of these will include basic responsibilities and educational requirements necessary for each position. Write your denominational headquarters and mission boards for information. Attend missionary appointment services. Attend summer assemblies where they discuss ministry or mission opportunities. Take time to discover some of your own interests and abilities by volunteering for different types of ministries. And don't forget to note your impressions in your journal or interview file. If possible, plan to take years to compile this information. Pieces of the puzzle will begin to fall into place as you go.

As you collect information about different vocations, be prayerful that the Spirit will begin revealing to you where God wants to use you. Note in your journal which ministries appeal to you and why, but don't try to select a position now. Remain open to the possibilities. You may find that God will use you in a number of different ministries throughout your lifetime.

Local Church Ministries

Pastor. The pastor is the proclaimer of God's Word as well as the under-shepherd for God's sheep. Major responsibilities include preaching, administration, pastoral care, evangelism, leading worship, and counseling. In small churches, duties may also include education, youth, and music. Educational requirements vary with churches and denominations, but the Master of Divinity degree is usually the preferred minimum.

Associate Pastor. An associate pastor works under the supervision and authority of a senior pastor. Responsibilities vary from church to church, but many associate pastors are given responsibility for counseling, hospital and evangelistic visitation, and filling the pulpit when the pastor is absent. Some churches use their associate pastors as specialized age-group ministers, calling them associate pastors instead of ministers of youth, and so forth. Educational requirements vary, depending on the job description, but master's level work is preferred.

Minister of Education. This person has ministry responsibilities in the area of Christian education. Major concerns are the teaching ministry of the church, outreach programs, age-group divisions, sponsoring committees, and other organizational matters. Many times this minister is also called upon to fill the pulpit, lead Bible studies and seminars, and aid in the counseling ministry. Again, educational requirements vary with the church and denomination, but most churches prefer a master's degree in Christian education or a related field.

Age-group Minister (e.g., of children, youth, singles, seniors). This church staff person has major responsibilities for all areas of ministry for a particular age-group. Administration, program planning, evangelism, counseling, Bible teaching, and even preaching are some of the responsibilities of the age-group minister. If you combine the work of a pastor and minister of education but limit that work to a particular age-group, you will have a good description of this ministry. Requirements for this position also vary, but most churches who can afford a full-time staff member prefer a person with master's level work in the area of specialty.*

---

*Many churches and denominations may also ask a prospective children or youth minister to send for a state criminal check and FBI child abuse clearance.

Minister of Preschool/Daycare. One of the newer ministry opportunities in recent years, this ministry encompasses the pre-school division of the church as well as the church's daycare/after-school programs. This minister must be knowledgeable in working with this age-group, qualified to train workers, and effec-tive in relating to parents as well. Management, organizational, and public relations skills are needed. Qualifications include a bachelor's or master's degree in early childhood education, and some states require teacher certification for the daycare di-rector in order for the facility to be licensed. State licensing boards also require a daycare to obtain FBI child abuse clear-ances and state criminal checks for all employees, including the director.

Minister of Music. The most obvious responsibilities are those dealing with the music program of the church. Music ministers may be expected to lead congregational singing, direct choirs and handbell groups, sing solos, and even provide accompaniment on the piano or organ. What many people may not realize, however, is the minister of music must also be a *minister* in the traditional sense. Counseling, visitation, and the pastoral care of those in the music ministry as well as in the church at large are oppor-tunities sometimes overlooked by music ministers. Qualifications in music are obviously needed, along with general ministry and organizational skills. Large churches who employ full-time music ministers prefer master's level training.

Director of Recreation. This minister works with the church staff to direct Christian recreation activities for all ages. He or she uses recreation as a tool for helping Christians grow in all as-pects of their lives. Many churches have built family life centers for their members, and the facilities offer outreach opportunities in their communities. Recreation directors are usually in charge of this facility, its scheduling, and its programs. Qualifications vary, but a degree in health, physical education, or church recre-ation is minimal, along with general organizational and ministry skills.

Church business administrator. The basic responsibility of this person is to manage the administrative and business affairs of a local church. Fortunate are the pastor and church who recognize the need for a person with the skills, training, and calling to fill this position. Too often pastors and other church staff — who should be working in their own areas of expertise — are burdened with responsibilities a church business administrator could do with ease. Qualifications include training and experience in business, accounting, finances, office management, property management, public relations, marketing, and/or communication. Bachelor's level education is minimal.

Church secretary/administrative assistant. Major responsibilities are largely clerical, including typing, filing, record keeping, answering telephones, and keeping staff calendars. Often the secretary is the public relations person for all who call or visit the church. Beyond these responsibilities, this person is expected to support the staff in any way possible to help the church run smoothly. Qualifications include basic office and public relations skills, as well as an understanding of church polity, the ability to keep confidences, and an awareness of the overall work of the church and the denomination. Larger churches often require more extensive clerical training and professional experience.

Combination minister. This person is responsible for more than one area of ministry in the church. Common combinations include: minister of music and youth, minister of education and music, minister of youth and children, minister of education and youth, and minister of all of the above! This Jack- or Jill-of-all-trades is asked to minister in a variety of ways with specific groups or ages. Many smaller churches that cannot afford multiple ministers will ask one person to handle multiple and diverse responsibilities. The major requirement for this position is flexibility! And, of course, the person filling this role must be trained (or willing to receive training) in the areas for which he or she is responsible. A bachelor's or master's degree is the usual level of education required for this type of position.

Mission/Denominational Work

Mission work. A common misconception concerning mission work is that it always involves preaching or medicine and that it must be done on the foreign field or in the inner cities of our country. In fact, with few exceptions, every ministry position that has already been described is also needed on the mission field, and the support ministries we tend to identify with overseas mission work are equally necessary on the home front.

Missions encompasses a broad range of ministries performed on different levels. The place of ministry may be in a local church, a regional assignment like the inner city, or the foreign mission field. The jobs vary, including church planting, evangelism, job training, administration, social services, preaching, construction, farming, counseling, and teaching. Some mission fields require trained professionals with special skills, such as translators, pilots, and civil engineers. Qualifications for mission work vary, depending on the position and the denomination, but adequate training in the area of responsibility, coupled with some theological education, is the minimum. God is ready to use anyone who is willing to build the Kingdom, whether here in North America or overseas. We simply need to be willing and available to the Spirit's call.

Denominational staff positions. There are numerous ministry positions available in denominational, state, or regional mission agencies and organizations. These administrative bodies are necessary so others can follow God's leading into "the field." Mission board staffs make it possible for missionaries to be appointed and supported. State board members assist church staff in their work and ministry. From the editor of the state newspaper to the traveling consultant, from the person who keeps the files on missionary candidates to the executive director of the mission board, all are serving as God-called ministers, faithful to God in their areas of ministry.

Qualifications are specific to the individual positions, but in addition to the skills necessary to carry out daily functions, commitment to God and the Spirit's ministry in the world should be a fundamental qualification of persons called to these jobs.

Specialty ministries. Many people feel called to use their training and expertise as "specialty ministers." These vocational positions include: drafters, architects, and contractors who design and build churches; artists and journalists who work for denominational agencies; editors and publishers of denominational curriculum; audiovisual technicians who prepare materials for churches and denominations; librarians who serve as consultants to churches or in Christian schools or agencies. The jobs are many and varied, and in most ways, they require the same training that is necessary for the person employed in comparable "secular" positions. The call is different, however: to serve God in a church-related agency or institution in areas where God has called us with the talents and tools God has provided.

Ministries outside the Local Church

Opportunities for ministry cover a much broader scope than you may realize. Most vocations may be accomplished on the home or foreign mission field, as a full-time, part-time, or bi-vocational minister. Moreover, many vocational Christian ministries do not take place in the local church at all. Some of these ministries are "Christian" positions in a secular environment; others use so-called secular training in a Christian environment. Examples of both types are described below.

Chaplain. You may feel called by God to fill a role as chaplain to a specific group or agency. Chaplains serve with the military and professional sports teams, in hospitals and prisons, in homes for children and for the aging. Even some corporations have chaplains available to their employees and clients for counsel and support. Qualifications include skills in counseling, pastoral care, and theology. A Master of Divinity is preferred, with special training in counseling and practical experience in ministry.

Student minister. "Diverse" describes the roles of campus ministers or directors of student ministry on college and university campuses, but all such ministers serve the student body as a friend, counselor, and administrator of religious programs and organizations. In many ways student ministers are campus pastors for students and staff. Qualifications usually include a Master of Divinity degree and experience in ministry.

Teacher/professor. Many people feel called to teach at church-affiliated schools, universities, seminaries, and divinity schools.

The primary responsibilities of the Christian educator are in the classroom, but they also serve on committees, pursue research and publication in their fields of study, and serve in their areas of expertise. Qualifications include training and experience in a field of expertise and, especially for graduate-level educators, a Ph.D. in the subject area.

Social service worker. Christians who are committed to social ministry may pursue training and education in social work, counseling, psychology, and the like and seek to use that training in Christian environments, both at home and on the foreign mission field. They are employed by churches, agencies, and homes for children or the elderly, or they may establish private practices on their own or with like-minded colleagues. Qualifications include adequate training in social ministry, the master's degree usually being the minimal level. Theological training is also necessary in many instances.

Medical professional. People trained in healthcare often feel called of God to use their training and abilities to serve the Lord in a full-time capacity. Physicians, nurses, medical technicians, and pharmacists are among those who respond to physical and spiritual need by committing their lives to a medical ministry in home and overseas missions. Qualifications include training in the medical field; theological training may be beneficial also.

How Can I Know What I Am to Do?

Although the question of "how do I know" is an important one, you may not need to ask it at this point in your search. The desire for clarity and certainty is natural and far from "wrong," but remember that this may not be the right time for God to show you the specifics of your vocation. Keep in mind these tips as you continue your search:

Take time to gather lots of information about a variety of vocations. Some of us settle for a lot less than God wants because we do not have enough information to make wise decisions. Some answers come only through training and experience. Ask questions of everyone you know who is involved in ministry. Ask if you can go with them as they minister. Watch them, and learn from them.

Try out various ministries as you have opportunity. Some of my students serve as youth ministers every summer instead of taking the opportunity to gain experience in other fields of service. You will learn a lot by trying areas of ministry that are completely new and different for you. Volunteer for various ministries, even on a small scale. Go to a children's home or a home for the aging, and lead a Bible study or devotion there. Teach Sunday school classes for a variety of age groups. If your church has a youth week each year, assume a leadership role for the week. Lead a children's choir or mission organization. Go on mission trips and to summer conferences. Ask your pastor to let you lead a prayer meeting or fill the pulpit. Ask the music director if you can lead choir practice one night.

Let others know of your search, and ask for their feedback. Don't assume you have to know all the specifics of God's will before you ask for others' prayers and guidance. You may have the impression that it is not okay to question others or search for God's will by asking people to pray for you. You may fear feeling humiliated later if you decide God is *not* calling you. However, until you can be open with others about your search, you are shutting the door to ways God may want to speak to you.

Whenever you try out a different ministry, ask other leaders or mature participants to observe you and write out an evaluation. For their convenience and yours, have an evaluation form already created that you can give to them. The form should include: (1) questions about the areas of strength they observed, (2) questions about areas where you need to grow or improve, and (3) space for them to offer general observations and suggestions. Ask your evaluators to be as candid as possible so that you can fully benefit from the experience.

Examine your own interests. If you absolutely hate to do something, that may be a good indication that God is *not* calling you to do that. God has created us with certain interests and abilities. We should not disregard these in our search.

According to one writer, interests are good indicators for a variety of reasons:

- Our interests reflect many of our basic human needs because these needs motivate us to act and to do things we like;

- Interests indicate what work will satisfy us, since we usually do what we enjoy; when work matches interests, it brings fulfillment instead of drudgery;

- Interests predict persistence in our work because we are willing to stick with what we enjoy;

- Our interests reflect conviction in our mission and purpose; and

- Interests are good indicators of God's gifts to us.[1]

Finally, work on your own growth as a person. If you take the time and effort needed to become all you can be on a daily basis, you can be more assured that you will be in the right place at the right time when you must make a decision about a specific career or vocation.

Self-Evaluation

In your journal or in discussion with a friend, consider the following questions.

1. Of all the specific vocations mentioned in this chapter, which one(s) appeal to you the most? Why?

2. In which "ministry activities" have you found the greatest personal satisfaction? What about those activities is fulfilling?

3. Have you given serious consideration to serving God on the foreign mission field? Why or why not?

4. Which ministry positions are you fairly certain are *not* where God wants to use you?

5. What other areas of ministry could you "try out" at this point in your life?

6. How do you feel about asking others to evaluate you in some ministry endeavor?

7. Who could you talk with in various ministry positions who could give you information on ministries that interest you?

8. If you could design the "perfect ministry" for yourself, what would it be? What would your role in it be?

Note

1. Felix E. Montgomery, *Pursuing God's Call: Choosing a Vocation in Ministry* (Nashville: Convention Press, 1981), 62.

Chapter Eight

EXPLORING BI-VOCATIONAL MINISTRY

"I've always wanted to be a math teacher, Dr. C." Terry shared one day when I asked him about his major. "But I also feel that God is calling me to preach. What should I do now?" he said, hoping I would have a prophetic answer to his dilemma.

"Have you ever considered that God may be wanting you to do both?" I asked, as I watched surprise and hope appear on his face. "Have you considered that the Lord may be calling you to be a dual career or bi-vocational minister?" I asked, inviting him to come into my office to discuss the possibilities.

As it turned out, Terry did wind up in a dual career ministry, and he is finding fulfillment in both areas of service. Perhaps you have never considered this possibility for your own life. You may be struggling with a call to ministry but have strong inclinations and interests in another career area. Your difficulty in making a decision may indicate that God wants you to do both, while you are trying to make a choice between the two. God does call many people into ministry areas that are considered "full-time," meaning the minister will have no other major means of financial support, but God calls others to minister bi-vocationally, alongside another career that will provide additional financial support. Unfortunately, we may fail to hear this unique call to dual career ministry because we don't have the necessary information. Therefore, before we examine this area of ministry, we should clarify a few terms and address some basic questions.

The phrases, "bi-vocational ministry," "dual career ministry," and "tent making" are often used to describe the same thing: a calling in which a person who serves in some type of ministry also works another job that provides financial support.[1] "Tent making" may imply a different shade of meaning for some people, who use it to refer to Christians who work in cross-cultural situations in jobs other than what the host culture would call "religious profession." The purpose and training of these believers is still missionary, but their means of support may be considered "secular." For our purposes, however, we will use the concept of "tent making" interchangeably with bi-vocational or dual career ministry.

Some of the questions we need to answer are: What makes bi-vocational ministry different from any other type of ministry? What kind of minister is a bi-vocational minister? Is this a new concept in ministry? What are some advantages and disadvantages of this type of ministry? How can I know if I am being called to minister in this way?

To get started, we will consider the history of this type of ministry. The Bible is a good place to begin our investigation.

A Biblical Look at Bi-Vocational Ministry

In the Old Testament we find many instances when the Lord called people to work toward holy purposes within their chosen occupations. Amos was a shepherd and dresser of sycamore trees as well as a prophet (Amos 7:14). Gideon threshed wheat and served as a judge and military ruler for God's people (Judges 6:11). Hosea may have worked in the bakery with his father and was used of God to speak to wayward Israel (Hosea 1, 3). Daniel was a prophet for God while working as a high ranking official in the government (Daniel 6). Nehemiah was a governor while undertaking the rebuilding of the temple (Nehemiah 4, 5); David was first a shepherd and then a king while serving God (1 Samuel 16:19; 2 Samuel 2:4).

Of course, there are also ample examples of Old Testament characters who served exclusively in the occupation of priest and/or prophet. The Lord did not rate one ministry higher or more holy than another. God called individuals to a work of God's own choosing; they were obedient to the call.

The New Testament records several examples of people who served God in ministry while working in another profession as a means of financial support. Luke may be considered a bi-vocational physician/evangelist. The apostle Paul mentioned Zenas the lawyer (Titus 3:13). Barnabas probably supported himself throughout his missionary career; we know he did so while working with Paul (1 Corinthians 9:6). Priscilla and Aquila were tent makers as they served and ministered for God (Acts 18:2–3); in fact, they taught the trade to Paul, who is probably the best-known example of bi-vocationalism in the New Testament.

Throughout his letters, Paul noted some of the reasons for wanting to support himself this way. He did not want to hinder the gospel (1 Corinthians 8:12). He did not want to be accused of preaching just for the financial rewards, as some apparently were doing (1 Corinthians 8:13). He did not want to be a burden to any church (2 Corinthians 11:9). Although he believed that church support of God's ministers was legitimate (1 Corinthians 9:1–14), he wanted to be a model, teaching that manual labor was not to be avoided.

Perhaps the most important lessons we can learn about tent making from the apostle Paul is that he believed it was God who supplied all his needs, regardless of the means of doing so. Beyond his own earnings from tent making, Paul also received support from churches he served. "The bi-vocational minister doesn't believe that full-time church financial support is any more of God than personal financial support. . . . The self-supporting pastor trusts God for support as much as the full-time pastor does."[2]

Historical Background

Ample evidence supports the concept that most clergy in the first few centuries worked to support themselves. From the days of the first-century church until the founding of our nation, nearly all ministers earned their livings with a skilled occupation.[3]

During the time of the monastic orders (A.D. 500–1500), manual labor was the accepted practice of those in the order. Some ministers during this time did receive support from their churches, but many refused it. Benedict of Nursia (543), St. Francis of Assisi (1223), and John Wycliffe (1350), all held to the belief that no one should receive money for the ministry they performed for God.[4]

During the Reformation, many preachers and church leaders were excluded from the blessing of the established church. The new churches were led by clergy "outside of apostolic succession."[5] Thus the bi-vocational minister arose out of necessity since the new congregations were small and could not support their pastors financially.

One of the earliest Protestant mission movements was led by the Moravians in the seventeenth century. All of their missionaries supported themselves by working in a secular occupation.[6] During the seventeenth and eighteenth centuries in America, people who went to the frontier supported themselves in many ways, sometimes serving as farmers or teachers as well as ministers.[7]

The father of the modern Protestant mission movement, William Cary, who left England in 1791 to go to India, was also a "tent maker." He worked many different jobs in order to support himself and his ministry. Shoemaker, naturalist, professor of oriental languages, and government translator are some of the hats he wore to support his own mission endeavors.[8]

Because today so many people serve God in a ministry vocation as their sole means of financial support, bi-vocational ministers are often treated as second-class servants. This is not the case! Dual career ministry is *not* a new or second-class option. Through the ages, God has repeatedly called and used people in ministry who supported themselves financially through other professions. People become bi-vocational ministers because they feel God has called them to use that strategy for reaching and serving people who might otherwise not be served.

Advantages of Bi-Vocational Ministry

You might ask, How could there possibly be any advantage to working two jobs? Other than being certain of an extra paycheck, why in the world would anyone want to take on that additional burden? When a person doesn't have time for one job, how could he or she possibly handle two? These are valid questions as we examine the possibility of dual career ministry. Let's take a look at some of the advantages of serving God this way. Most of these answers were given by those who have served in this capacity.

This type of ministry enables some churches to have staff they otherwise could not afford if full financial support were required. The small church where I served as bi-vocational minister of education for 10 years only had 200 members in Sunday school. The church could not possibly afford a full-time minister of education. But since I was bi-vocational and teaching at a university provided my major means of support, this small church was able to have a staff member who had a Ph.D. in the field, something usually only large churches can afford.

When a pastor or other staff member is self-supporting, budget money is freed for use in other areas of need. Many times the tithes and offerings the bi-vocational staff member gives to the church amount to more than the salary they are receiving from the church.

Tent making is a means of financial support for the person who is commissioned as a church planter, to begin a church in an area where there are few or none. No denomination has the resources necessary to support missionaries everywhere in our country and overseas that need a gospel witness. God calls men and women to join the mission of reaching a lost world, and many of those workers will be laypersons or bi-vocational ministers who will support themselves financially as they spread the gospel.

Many church members will accept greater responsibilities for the work of the church when the staff are bi-vocational. When church members realize their staff cannot do all of the work of ministry because they work other jobs, congregations find the incentive to exercise their own ministry gifts. In the church I mentioned before, where I served bi-vocationally for ten years, my goal was to train the lay leaders so well that I would work myself out of a job. And that is exactly what happened. When I felt God leading me away from the church, the church felt it was prepared to shoulder the responsibilities I had once held, so the members voted to eliminate the position!

Being a bi-vocational minister allows the person to experience the joy of serving in a fulfilling secular occupation. Many people have special talents and interests that draw them into other lines of work, even though they have felt the call of God on their lives. When discussing foreign mission possibilities with my students, I often observe that there are almost as many ways to serve God in missions as there are "secular" jobs in our society. Teachers, farmers, doctors, nurses, architects, business people, pilots, translators, graphic artists, computer programmers — the list goes on. Even many areas in our own country do not have a gospel witness because we fail to hear God's call to go and work in the fields, some of us being supported by secular jobs.

Bi-vocational ministries afford people opportunities to grow and succeed in ways full-time ministry may not provide. To the individual ministering in a small church where the struggles often outweigh present rewards, a secular vocation may offer much needed personal fulfillment in the form of advancement, competition, awards, and recognition. When we do succeed in our secular pursuits, our church members rejoice with us. I remember how proud my church family was when I was selected as Teacher of the Year at my university.

Another plus for bi-vocational ministry is the relationships you can develop outside the church. One of the most difficult things a staff member and his or her family must face is whether to become close friends with certain members of the church. Problems often arise when jealousy or church conflicts become an issue. And when full-time ministers leave their position, they often must leave behind the only support system they have.

Bi-vocational ministers are able to make more adequate

provision for their families. Many full-time ministers are burdened with low salaries or forced resignations. The bi-vocational
minister has a sense of independence that is liberating, for both
the minister and family. The spouse may choose not to work.
The family has an opportunity to own their own home. Children
have the opportunity to stay in one community and its schools.

*The dual career minister finds a welcomed diversion in two
jobs*. This diversion facilitates a better perspective on both areas
since the minister is able to get away from each job for some
period of time each week. In some ways a secular job provides
a reprieve from responsibilities as a church staff person. Becoming a "regular person" is not only a relief from vocational stress;
it enables the minister to understand the pressures the church
members face. A bi-vocational minister is less tempted to become
an "ivory tower preacher."

*Bi-vocational ministry tends to remove the distinction between
the secular and the religious*. This perspective of ministry as en-
compassing all of life will inevitably have an effect on the laity of
the church. For the bi-vocational minister and his or her congregation, ministry can become a part of everyday life, not just an
activity that must be planned. This perspective, when wedded to
the secular work environment, often fosters unique opportunities
for ministry and evangelism not afforded the full-time minister.
And when the pastor mentions in a sermon how he or she overcame a difficulty at work or witnessed to someone on the job,
that testimony can give added impetus to the congregation to do
the same.

*Some small churches may not require enough of their staff
members to utilize all their abilities*. "A ten-talented bi-vocational
person can avoid being underemployed by working two jobs."[9]
Pastor, staff member, and laity find it too easy to surrender their
responsibilities and grow lazy if the church is too small to need
a full-time minister. Some churches fall into the trap of compar-
ing their own organization with other churches'. Then they feel
second-rate if they do not have the same staff another church
has. In God's kingdom, quantity is far less important than quality.

The family of a bi-vocational minister is often treated more like a regular community family. Children who live in a different community from the church may escape the constant pressure and scrutiny of some church members. The bi-vocational family can maintain a healthy distance and be a team that serves the church, rather than a family owned by the church.

The dual career minister will bring people, materials, and ideas from areas outside the traditional sources.[10] These ideas can add to the ones the church receives from denominational and associational offices. The external perspective will be a valuable supplement to the information that comes from the regular channels.

Another plus to bi-vocational ministry is long tenure. "Generally, if the bi-vocational pastor has served a particular congregation two years or more and relationships are good, he [or she] can remain as long as he [or she] feels led to stay."[11] In contrast, statistics in many denominations reveal the average length of stay for a full-time pastor or staff member is less than two years.

Disadvantages of Bi-Vocational Ministry

Of course, there are also disadvantages in serving as a dual career minister, and if you are exploring this type of ministry, you should carefully consider the cons as well as the pros before making a decision. Surveys and discussions with people in bi-vocational ministry have identified a number of difficulties, which appear to fall into two categories.

Perhaps the most obvious difficulty is the matter of time. Finding enough time for both vocations, family, and personal hobbies and relaxation is incredibly difficult. Your stress level can be extremely high, especially if you have not developed good time management skills. Stress may be magnified by a personal need to succeed in every endeavor — which leads to the second common problem for bi-vocational ministers: self-esteem. As a bi-vocational minister, you must be satisfied with doing the best you can, even if that means leaving some things undone or failing to satisfy everyone you serve, at the church or on the secular job.

These two "problem areas" for the bi-vocational minister should be considered more closely.

Time

Scheduling conflicts are a perennial problem for bi-vocational ministers. There is never enough time to do all that needs to be done. Many times the family members of the dual career minister are the ones who suffer. Tent makers themselves often complain of physical fatigue and emotional and spiritual exhaustion. They experience great frustration when they hear people at their secular jobs express thanks for the upcoming weekend, when they know they look forward to more work and no time for relaxation. Dual career ministers absolutely must learn to make time for themselves and for their families.

Beyond those two priorities, many bi-vocational ministers express disappointment at not being able to be more available for the pastoral needs of the congregation, such as funerals, weddings, and counseling. They don't have time to be active in denominational activities or training opportunities. They feel left out of professional associations, pastors' conferences, conventions, and other occasions when full-time ministers meet. Because bi-vocational ministers seldom hold offices in denominational organizations or serve on agency boards, they may feel marginalized, left out of the center of ministerial life. Conversely, other dual career ministers feel trapped in one church because they live and work in that community, although this seems to be more of a problem with the pastoral role than secondary staff positions.

In a very practical sense, the crisis of finding time to do two jobs well can place bi-vocational ministers at a distinct disadvantage. Many live with the sense of "running in and doing my ministry and then having to leave." Some fall into a rut because they lack the time to be creative. They rely on past successes and methodologies because they do not have time to learn different ways of doing the job. Sometimes the road of least resistance is tempting. When tempted, however, the dual career minister would be wise to remember that any job worth doing is worth doing well.

The road of least resistance beckons not only in practical, task-oriented ways; problematic relationships within the church may tempt the dual career minister to dash in and out, dealing with conflict or tension in a superficial way at best. This is even more of a temptation to bi-vocational ministers because of the independence afforded them. They may be more successful in running from difficulties in the church, when they ought to commit the time and energy to work through the problems. Bi-vocational ministers may also find it easier to rationalize why certain things are not being done by using that second job as an excuse.

Self-Esteem

Since some people think dual career ministry is second-rate, the person in such a role often hears such insensitive remarks as: "When are you going into real ministry?" or "Aren't you good enough to be hired by a large church?" If you intend to pursue dual career ministry, you must know beyond a doubt that you have been called to the role. Otherwise, you will always have a nagging thought of having fallen short of God's will. Some bi-vocational ministers live with that self-doubt, wondering if they have faith enough to do ministry without earning a second income. Some fear they may be taking the easy and secure way out but are falling short of God's best. Some live with the frustration of never being called to "First Church." Again, it is essential that you be *sure* you are called to a dual vocation before deciding to serve in such a role; otherwise, you *may* be settling for second best when God wants you to trust the Lord to supply your needs.

Another common self-esteem problem in bi-vocational ministry is role confusion. In some ways dual career ministers are members of the clergy; in other ways they feel like members of the laity. When they are at church, they are in charge. But when they are on the job, they may be regarded simply as another employee. This disjunction can lead to role confusion and other problems. A pastor who has little control in his secular role may become controlling in the pastoral role.

Some bi-vocational ministers who pastor churches express their frustration in *not* being accepted at their workplaces as just another employee. When the knowledge of their ministerial role becomes known, they experience discrimination and pressure they had not felt before taking up the second role. Co-workers expect more out of them and are less tolerant of their weaknesses. These bi-vocational ministers also feel pressure to act as "pastors" even in the secular workplace.[12]

Some bi-vocational ministers experience disillusionment when they compare their church members with the people with whom they work; perhaps members are far less Christlike than non-Christian co-workers, or they have less commitment or inferior business sense. In whatever way(s) the church members fall short, the resultant disillusionment often affects the ministers' own sense of self-confidence and self-worth.

Many dual career ministers express frustration because their churches seem satisfied to stay as they are, "ossified in their old-time way of doing things." This causes the bi-vocational minister to wonder if a full-time minister would come with a different perspective and effect a needed change.[13]

Another critical area in the life of a bi-vocational minister is what has been called the "past fifties complex."[14] This is the time when dual career ministers realize they cannot continue to do all they have been able to do in the past. Recovery and recuperation take longer; tasks require more energy than is available. The dual role becomes too much. Wise ministers will renegotiate their contract, learn how to delegate more responsibilities, or decide to retire from one of the responsibilities. If the bi-vocational minister is unable or unwilling to accept this reality gracefully, the effects on the church and on the minister's self-esteem can be disastrous.

Self-Assessment

Maturity is essential in a dual career ministry. You must learn how to delegate to others, to plan your time wisely, to organize all aspects of your life, and to be a team player. You must be willing to set limits, face your own strengths and weaknesses, allow room for mistakes, and learn how to deal with failure. Good health habits are essential. Practice spiritual disciplines to keep your spiritual life strong. Set your priorities and keep your focus if you hope to be successful and effective as a dual career minister.

If you and I are to be faithful as well as fruitful in our roles as bi-vocational ministers, we must be certain the Lord has called us to fill this role. The alternative will be disastrous.

Examine carefully your own feelings about bi-vocational ministry. Write in your journal or discuss with someone the thoughts that arise as you consider the following questions.

In the past, have you thought of bi-vocational ministry as being "second-rate" in contrast to full-time ministry? Do you worry that other Christians will look down on you for being a dual career minister? Have you ever considered being a bi-vocational minister? Are you willing to consider a dual career calling? Do you know any bi-vocational ministers with whom you could talk, to learn about their experiences, both positive and negative? Do you think you could find fulfillment as a "tent maker"? Consider in what vocation you might enjoy working, alongside your ministry.

Notes

1. J. W. Bargiol, "The Bi-vocational Pastor," *Church Administration* (March 1987): 12.

2. Luther M. Dorr, *The Bivocational Pastor* (Nashville: Broadman, 1988), 15.

3. Ibid., 21–22.

4. Ibid., 23.

5. John Y. Elliott, *Our Pastor Has an Outside Job* (Valley Forge, Pa.: Judson Press, 1980), 18.

6. Ibid., 11.

7. Ibid., 18–19.

8. Don Hamilton, *Tentmakers Speak* (Ventura: Regal Books, 1987), 10.

9. Dorr, 65.

10. David W. Hayes, "The Bi-vocational Minister of Youth," *Church Administration* (March 1987): 22.

11. Bargiol, 13.

12. Gary Farley, "The Bi-vocational Minister," *Search* (Summer 1977): 62.

13. Ibid., 60.

14. Bargiol, 14.

Chapter Nine

WHERE DO I GO FROM HERE?

I was in Houston for an In-Service Guidance Association meeting. Having difficulty locating the motel where I was to stay, I stopped at a gas station to ask directions. I placed my map of the city on the counter so the attendant could point out where the motel was located.

"It's not too far from here," he assured me, drawing a circle around the place on the map. "Just go straight about five miles, take a right, go three miles, take a left, and you can't miss it," he added, turning to assist another customer who had just walked in.

If he only knew how easy it is for me to get lost, he may not have been quite so certain I wouldn't miss it! But as I turned to walk out, I quickly remembered one strategic thing. I walked back into the station and approached the counter again. "Sir, do you mind telling me where I am now?"

As soon as the question came out of my mouth, he and I both burst into laughter. "I guess that's the problem with a lot of folks, isn't it?" he said, taking the map once more in his hands. He drew another circle marking the place where his station was located and walked over to the door. "There is the road you are to get on. Turn right and you are on your way."

I thanked him, still laughing under my breath, but realizing once again there are spiritual truths everywhere if we will only look for them.

I have pondered on that particular incident many times. Many of us might have questions about God's leadership because we are not sure where we are now. We need to understand where we are *now* before we can make much progress. Through reading this book, discussing it with trusted friends, and reflecting on other experiences you have with God, you may be gaining insight into your present situation. Hopefully you are at the point of asking, "Where do I go from here?" Consider some of the following possibilities.

If You Know God Has Called You to Ministry

If you feel fairly confident that God has called you to ministry, then you are embarking on the most exciting journey of your life. But there are some important things you should keep in mind as you travel.

Never be more concerned about God's call on your life than you are about your relationship with the One who has called you. As exciting as it is to know that God has placed a hand upon us to do a special work, sometimes we are tempted to go ahead with plans for working out that calling, and we forget to maintain a vital relationship with the Caller. So, keep your spiritual disciplines high on your priority list. Daily Bible study and prayer are absolutely necessary if you are going to maintain a close walk with God. Remember: it is difficult, if not impossible, to lead others deeper in their relationship with God than you yourself have gone. Spiritual burnout is a very real possibility if you are giving out more than you are taking in.

Begin to minister and exercise your calling and your spiritual gifts now. Do not wait until you complete your formal education before you begin what God has called you to do. Many of your most valuable lessons will be learned in "on the job training." Ask your church to let you serve in any way you can. If you live on a campus, look for opportunities to serve those you are around each day, even your professors! Volunteer for events and organizations that will let you gain ministry experience. Deliberately expose yourself to a variety of ministry experiences. Many of us limit God's call on our lives because we do not get exposure to different ministries. Hundreds of Christian ministry opportunities are available today, many more than the traditional vocations of the pastorate, missions, and youth, education, and music ministries. Often God will clarify our calls when we are "trying out" these different ministries. I like to think of it as "gathering puzzle pieces." The problem is *not* that God is trying to make a puzzle out of our calling; rather, we cannot understand God's will except one piece at a time.

When I was called to Christian ministry, I was nineteen and had been a Christian for only one year. I was so grateful that God had saved me, I was willing to do whatever the Lord wanted. Instead I found that God said, "I want *you*" — not much more information than that. As I look back now, I can understand why. I have been involved in three different full-time Christian ministries since that initial calling: as minister of music and education in a local church, as consultant on a state convention staff, and as professor at a Baptist university. I have also served bi-vocationally. How could God have communicated all of that when I was nineteen? The complexity of the call would have scared me to death!

My experiences have taught me that, when gathering the puzzle pieces of God's call, I need to walk with God one step at a time. I have a tendency to be independent and to attempt to work out God's plans in my own strength. God knows that I am better off taking one day at a time — and now I know it too! Of course, that does not mean I don't wish I could see farther down the road sometimes!

In addition to pursuing "on the job training," you will need to dedicate yourself in the classroom. This applies equally to your undergraduate education, graduate studies, and seminary course work. God wants you to take your academic training seriously, even if you cannot understand what difference a math or English course is going to make when you are working in a church or on the mission field. You may ask, "How can I be expected to make good grades when I am so busy serving God? I am in a hurry to get out there and win souls for Jesus."

Whenever I encounter students with this impatience to serve,

I remind them that Jesus worked faithfully in his earthly father's carpentry shop before he began his heavenly Father's work full-time. I ask them to consider how earnestly he must have worked as a carpenter, while waiting for God's will to unfold. I ask if they think the work that Jesus did was haphazard because he was anxious to get out there and minister to the world. I believe that he did everything, even carpentry, as well as he possibly could. Perhaps his woodworking was a means of ministering to others while he waited and prepared for his teaching ministry. Perhaps carpentry taught him lessons that came in handy in his ministry: patience, strength of body, gentleness of hands, appreciation for the process, and understanding for how the people to whom he later ministered lived. In the same way, you should use your time in academic training, not only for learning theory but for building character and seizing every opportunity to minister to fellow students, faculty, and staff.

I cannot imagine Jesus having the same kind of impatience we have. Could it be that the greatest ministry, and perhaps the only ministry for some, is what they will accomplish while they are still in school? You may be tempted to dream about "the great ministry" you will do "someday" and completely miss the ministry opportunities God places in front of you today. Ask yourself: "If I were to die the day after I graduated, would others say I had missed the ministry? Or would they say I was a great minister while I was in school with them?"

Let your church family know of your decision to pursue vocational ministry. Their prayers, encouragement, and even financial support will be immeasurably helpful to you. And if they know how you think God is leading you, they will more likely let you minister to and "practice on them." Gather a support group, from your local church and beyond; include people who are studying for the ministry and others who are already in the ministry. As you may have already discovered, you will have days when you doubt your calling and are tempted to quit. On those days especially, you will need a group that can encourage and support you. The fire of your call will be less likely to go out if it has the warmth from the flames of others to feed it and keep it aglow.

Be as active in a local church as you would expect others to be if you become a pastor or other staff member. Of course, the extent of your involvement may depend on your current responsibilities as a student, but even while in school, keep your church attendance active. And don't be a "cafeteria member" — one who goes to this church and then that one, depending upon who is "serving up" what. Join a church where you are going to school, and volunteer to do some ministry in it.

If the church you are attending doesn't need you (although this is hard for me to believe!), volunteer for some ministry in your community. For example, when I was a student, I went to a nursing home once a week and led singing and Bible study. Many colleges and seminaries have their own ministry projects in which you might become involved — in anything from a student chaplain program to a local chapter of Habitat for Humanity. All of us need to be ministering in some way to others even when we are primarily students.

If you have an opportunity to serve as a student pastor, youth worker, or in a similar staff position during your student days, do so even if the ministry is only for the summer months. The experiences you gain will be valuable "pieces of the puzzle," and you will be developing valuable ministry experiences. Nearly all employers — whether churches or community groups — prefer to hire people who have had some hands-on ministry experience. Even after you complete any required practicums or internships at your school, remain active in some form of ministry. You need to be "giving out" as well as "taking in" during these days of training. If you give out more than you take in, you will burn out. If you take in more than you give out, you will stagnate — "the dead sea syndrome." You should avoid both extremes.

Remain as open as possible to God's leadership at every juncture. Don't draw a geographical circle around yourself and limit yourself to going to school or serving only within one hundred miles of your hometown. God is looking for servants who are willing go anywhere and do anything. If you begin to limit God in small things — such as where you are willing to go to school or what courses you will take — you are more likely to limit

God in the bigger things as well. Ask God to give you the faith that Abraham had, being willing to step out in obedience, "even though he did not know where he was going" (Hebrews 11:8). Then we are much more likely *not* to limit what God wants to do for, in, and through us.

Finally, keep a journal, especially of the ways God speaks to you and leads you. You can look back at it and gain valuable insight about how God usually deals with you. Since the Lord relates to us all as individuals and speaks to us in different ways, you should seek to discover specific patterns in how you have heard God's voice in your own life. Then when you are at a crossroads and a decision has to be made, you can look back at past patterns and find insights for discerning God's call in the present. One pattern I have noticed in my own life is that God usually makes me feel dissatisfied with my present circumstances just prior to opening another door of opportunity.

Some of you may be disciplined enough to keep a daily journal of your thoughts, feelings, activities, and spiritual pilgrimage. This is a great habit to develop. But even if you do not keep a daily journal, at least record those special spiritual experiences you have with God, which are places where you should "build an altar." "Go back to Bethel" often and remember. These times of reflection will help you during days of darkness and confusion and allow you to recognize the voice of God as the Spirit speaks to you.

What If I Am Still Unsure?

I served for over twenty years with Dr. Logan Carson, a professor of Old Testament who was blind. Naturally he was an inspiration to all of us in the department and to the students who were privileged to be in his classes. He had developed his sense of hearing to help compensate for his lack of sight. He could recognize people not only by their voices but by their footsteps. On many occasions as a student entered his classroom (or tried to sneak out), he would stop what he was saying and call him or her by name. Many students and staff, including me, often wondered if he could really see!

On many occasions I led him to certain places on campus and assisted him as the faculty processed in a graduation ceremony. He would lightly touch my shoulder and walk just one-half step behind me. Whenever we approached steps or something else that might cause him difficulty, I would let him know what was ahead. Otherwise, he simply followed behind me, confident that I was leading him safely. After he became familiar with a terrain, he could and would navigate by himself, without even using a cane. When someone gave him a ride home, he was able to tell where they were and when it was time to make a turn. He was discerning enough to know when he needed help and when he was able to act without assistance.

Although most of us are not physically blind, all of us experience times of "spiritual blindness," when we cannot see where the Spirit is leading or what God is trying to show us. At these times, we can continue to walk by faith, counting on our heavenly Guide to give us directions when we need them. The longer we walk in that trust, the more confident we will become, in our Guide and in our own ability to discern the way of faith.

Take note of the following guidelines, which can serve as trail markers when the way is unclear and you cannot see where you are going.

Keep your spiritual disciplines healthy. As you pray and study your Bible, you will become more familiar with how the Lord speaks. You need to have a vital relationship with God first; your concern about a vocation should always be secondary to this.

Discover and use your spiritual gifts in ministry now. Use every opportunity you have to try out different ministries. Many times the Lord uses those experiences to confirm a ministry or help you understand what you do *not* want to do. Just as important as discovering what you *are* called to do is finding out what you are *not* gifted to do.

Do not create a ministry in your mind and talk yourself into being called to it. Perhaps you have admired a pastor or youth minister and want to serve in this kind of ministry because of what that person meant to you. God may use experiences and relationships such as those to lead you in a particular direction, but you need to be careful that *God* is leading and not your own desires.

Don't wait until you have all the answers before you begin the journey. Some people are "stuck on first base" because they do not know where home plate is. Go ahead and do what you *do know,* and God will give you the guidance you need for the next step.

Talk with others who have answered the call to ministry. Talk with some who have recently heard the call as well as some who have been in the ministry for many years. Don't expect your experience to be exactly like anyone else's, but be open to hear if God speaks to you through another's testimony.

Ask your church to pray for you. Relate to the congregation you desire to follow God's direction. Be sure to tell them you are still searching for God's will for your life. If you lead them to believe you are called to ministry and later realize otherwise, some people may think you have forsaken the call. And you would *not* want to go into the ministry simply to keep from disappointing family, friends, or church members.

Be certain not to confuse the call to discipleship with the call to ministry. Work on your relationship with God so you can know Christ is Lord of your life and that you are daily walking in obedience to him. When you establish a healthy relationship with the Lord, you are more likely to understand when and if God wants you to serve in vocational ministry.

Do not think you are settling for a second-rate ministry if you feel that God is leading you to be a bi-vocational minister. In case you are ever tempted to think this, remember that the apostle Paul, one of God's greatest ministers, was also a tent maker. The major thing you should be concerned about is what God wants *you* to do.

Remember that God may have a number of "jobs" or ministries for you to do before the Lord is finished with you. Concentrate on being the best you can be for God now. Don't be tempted to think that things would be so much better for you if you only knew the future. God may be trying to get you to trust, one step at a time.

As I was rereading this chapter, sitting at home in my study, my Shih Tzu jumped into my lap, curled up, and fell asleep. As I handwrite this paragraph, he is curled up with his head snuggled in my left arm, snoring away contentedly. He knows I won't do anything to hurt him; his trust is complete. So must ours be in our wonderful Lord who keeps us in God's care. "Do not be afraid, little flock, for your Father has been pleased to give you the kingdom" (Luke 12:32). Can you trust God with your life?

CONCLUSION

Jim loved playing trumpet in the high school band. He found particular joy during the football season when the band performed during half time. It was a challenge to him to play the music correctly while staying in step with the band. The formations were especially difficult this year, but he was determined to do his part to make the school proud of its marching band.

It was time for the homecoming game against the school's chief rival. The band had practiced its drills every afternoon that week. But the night before the big game, someone broke into the band room and changed all the marching directions except in Jim's folder and the director's.

Half time arrived, and the band took its position on the field. No one suspected anything. But halfway through the performance, the director blew his whistle, and made a sharp right turn. Jim's instructions indicated the right turn, but everyone else turned left! There he was, the only one marching in the same direction as the band director. The rest of the band was marching in step, in perfect formation, in the opposite direction!

"What should I do?" Jim thought to himself. At just that moment, the director marched over next to Jim and said, "Just keep following me. Don't worry about what the others are doing." Slowly, but deliberately, the band director led Jim over to join the group to finish the performance.

Jim had mixed emotions. He wished he had not been the only one to leave the group, but he was glad he had followed the director. After the game, in the band room, Jim tried to explain to all his friends what had happened.

"We still love you, Jim. After all, you were the one who looked lost, not us!"

And the band director chimed in, "Well done, Jim. I was especially pleased that you carefully followed the directions you had before you. That is what really matters."

Some of you feel like Jim. You have been given directions that seem to be very different from the ones your friends have. They are walking in a different direction from the way you feel you must go. The Master Director encourages you to be faithful to your own instructions. Just keep following, and God will faithfully lead you and assure you one day with the words: "Well done, my good and faithful servant."

Jimmy exploded! He threw his toy truck on the floor! This was the third time this week. He was restless at school, and he was waking up two or three times every night. His mother couldn't understand why he had changed so. She was sure he was happy—after all, they were getting settled in their new home and their new church. His dog died three weeks ago but they were even replacing him. Why was Jimmy like this?

You guessed it—stress.

Kids experience stress a great deal more than we want to believe—they have as many problems as adults do. In this book we will see how we can help our children and our teens handle their stress

Dr. H. Norman Wright has also written

Crisis Counseling

Published by Here's Life Publishers

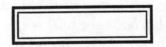

H. NORMAN WRIGHT

Helping Your Kids Handle

STRESS

Here's Life Publishers

First printing, October 1989

Published by
HERE'S LIFE PUBLISHERS, INC.
P. O. Box 1576
San Bernardino, CA 92402

Adapted from *Helping Teens Handle Stress* (© 1987) and *Helping Children Handle Stress* (© 1987), both by H. Norman Wright.

Printed in the United States of America, by Arcata Graphics/Kingsport, Kingsport, TN.

Library of Congress Cataloging-in-Publication Data
Wright, H. Norman.
     Helping your kids handle stress / H. Norman Wright.

       p.   cm.

     ISBN 0-89840-271-9

     1. Stress in children.   2. Stress management.
   3. Child rearing—religious aspects—Christianity.
   4. Children—Religious life.   5. Christian life—1960-
I. Title.

BF723.S75W765   1990

649'.1—dc20   89-27607
                                  CIP

For More Information, Write:
L.I.F.E.—P.O. Box A399, Sydney South 2000, Australia
Campus Crusade for Christ of Canada—Box 300, Vancouver, B.C., V6C 2X3, Canada
Campus Crusade for Christ—Pearl Assurance House, 4 Temple Row, Birmingham, B2 5HG, England
Lay Institute for Evangelism—P.O. Box 8786, Auckland 3, New Zealand
Campus Crusade for Christ—P.O. Box 240, Raffles City Post Office, Singapore 9117
Great Commission Movement of Nigeria—P.O. Box 500, Jos, Plateau State Nigeria, West Africa
Campus Crusade for Christ International—Arrowhead Springs, San Bernardino, CA 92414, U.S.A.

CONTENTS

87503

Bitter are the tears of a child:
    Sweeten them.
Deep are the thoughts of a child:
    Quiet them.
Soft is the heart of a child:
    Do not harden it.
    —*Lady Pamela Windham Glenconner*

THE WORLD OF KIDS

Jimmy exploded, and he threw his toy truck on the floor! This was the third time this week. He was restless at school, and he was waking up two or three times every night. His mother just couldn't understand why his behavior had changed so much. She was sure he was happy—after all, they were getting settled in their new home, and they finally had located a new church which would meet all their needs. This week they were even going to look for a new puppy to replace Jack, their collie who had died three weeks before. Why was Jimmy like this?

You guessed it—stress.

Kids experience stress a great deal more than we would like to believe. No matter what a child's age is, his world holds as many problems as an adult's. We may feel a child's stress is of less intensity or importance

than that of an adult, but that is not necessarily true. Children's trials can be especially traumatic for them, and can produce tragic long-term results. Troubled children need help in handling stress, and the sooner we can give them that help, the better chance they will have to grow and develop into emotionally healthy and mature individuals. In this book we'll examine several aspects of stress that occur in childhood and during the teen years, and we will look at a number of things we can do to help our children cope with that stress.

Early Childhood—The "Magic Years"

Part of the process of understanding and helping a child handle stress is understanding how a child thinks and how he perceives life. Early childhood has been called the "magic years." The ages of three to six make up this time period. We call this the time of magical thinking because at this stage the child thinks he is omnipotent. He believes he is at the center of life and can affect what happens—he believes that his own thought process can influence objects and events in the world outside himself.

Because of this, he is unable to understand why his pet dies, or why he can't have what he wants when he wants it, or why he gets sick. He becomes disturbed with unfamiliar bodily changes that accompany illness, and he often believes he caused the illness. Sometimes he feels he was bad or something is defective about him and that's why something bad happened to him. He does not perceive life as unpredictable. We adults accept sudden events as part of life. In fact, Scripture teaches us that life is uncertain and we should expect problems and upsets to occur, but a child has difficulty grasping this.

Because young children are egocentric (centered on themselves), they fail to consider the viewpoints of others. This has nothing to do with being conceited; it is just a normal part of the developmental process. They take things for granted and do not realize that other people need clarification. It's not until a child reaches the age of about seven that he begins to distinguish between his perspective and someone else's.

Three- to six-year-olds talk past one another. They have their own private speech and may not be talking to anyone in particular. They are not concerned whether you understand their words or not. They just assume their words have more meaning than is there.

A young child takes things at face value—literally. When a parent says, "I'm sick and tired of the way you are acting," what does a child think? He catches the parent's anger, but he also believes the parent actually may be getting both "sick" and "tired."

Think of other phrases we say that can be misunderstood: "Keep your shirt on"; "Hold your horses"; "That's cool"; and so on. Try to enter the child's mind. If you could hear what he is thinking, you would be amazed!

A child puts two and two together and does not necessarily come up with four. His unique connections make sense to him but to no one else. A child may see illness and going to the football game as related because his father became seriously ill the last time he went to a football game. A child may even become anxious and avoid going to a game because of the connection he made.

When Brad was about six, he injured himself on the jungle gym at school, but he refused to tell his mother what had happened to him. After several days

of questioning, all she could get him to say was, "I can't tell you." Over and over he would repeat this, sometimes even in tears. His mother was becoming increasingly alarmed over what really had happened to him until she began to make a connection. A friend of hers had died in a hospital just recently. Her son, she discovered, was afraid that if he told her what had happened, he would have to go to a hospital, and—in his mind—if he did, he would die.

Middle Childhood

For children of all ages, stressors vary in their intensity. In the middle childhood years, different degrees of stress can be felt from such things as a poor grade on a test, the loss of a pet frog, rejection or ridicule by a friend, moving, or the separation or divorce of parents. And remember—children are more limited in their coping than adults. They don't have the repertoire of experiences to draw upon when faced with stressors and some of these things can be extremely difficult for a child to cope with.

Travel back in time with me and picture yourself as a seven-year-old child. You and your parents have just moved, and this is your first day at a new school in the middle of a semester. You didn't sleep well last night. Your stomach doesn't feel good, and you have to go to the bathroom a lot.

As you walk down the hall to your new classroom, you see other children looking at you. Some of them are giggling. You feel like turning around and running. You open the classroom door and thirty strange faces turn around and stare at you. Your heart rate increases and your stomach tightens up. The teacher makes you the focus of attention by telling the class that

you are the new student, and then she proceeds to ask you your name. But the words just won't come out of your mouth! That is stress! Do you remember what it was like?

Children from seven to twelve have changed considerably in their thinking. They have advanced in their ability to think conceptually. They are now able to work out some problems in their heads instead of just by trial and error. They can see the viewpoints of other people, and they recognize the feelings of others as well. Even their world of fantasy has changed. They now fantasize about real people and events instead of engaging in so much make-believe. They can make sense of stress.

Children in the middle years are usually enjoyable and uncomplicated, calm and educable, but they still have a difficult time dealing with anything that resembles intense stress. They prefer to avoid the issue and often will change the subject when you attempt to draw them into a discussion of their problems. They try to avoid the pain and anxiety. This is why so many people who work with children of this age use games and play in the therapy process. Play allows children an outlet for what they are feeling and gives the counselor the information sought. Communication toys such as tape recorders, phones, drawing materials and puppets are very helpful.

However, even though these children have developed considerably in their thinking processes, they still tend to jump to conclusions without considering all the facts. Actually, children of this age group have a tendency to listen to contradictory information and not see the inconsistency. They often do not understand what they are hearing. Sometimes these children will not understand adults who are talking to them, and another

real problem is that the adults often do not realize they are not being understood.

Teenagers

As for teenagers, have you ever tried to talk to one and in exasperation found yourself asking, "Are you deaf?" because you got no answer? Don't feel alone!

Parents of teenagers everywhere are realizing that teens live in their own world, a world inside themselves. They are self-centered, and they often withdraw from contact with others.

They regard themselves as unique and special, and they tend to live in a state of either agony or ecstasy! Their subjectivity level is high. They are self-critical, and they assume others are critical of them, too. They become super-sensitive and are subject to quick shame and dramatic embarrassment. Social pressures peak and self-doubt and feelings of inferiority intensify.

Unfortunately, a teen's self-worth is nearly always dependent upon one of the most unstable pillars in existence — peer acceptance. One unstable group is trying to gain stability from another unstable group.

In answer to the question, "What is a teenager?" Bettie Youngs gives a thorough description in her book, *Helping Your Teenager Deal With Stress.*

1. The teen is a person who is leaving childhood and working through the stages of adolescence.

2. When this person is frightened, he (or she) tends to regress to the security of being a child and may behave accordingly.

3. Rapid and intense physiological and psychological changes are occurring.

4. The teenager desperately yearns for inde-

pendence, but does not have enough experience to be independent.

5. Teenagers have a great desire to express personal needs and to be taken seriously.

6. They have not yet firmly established their own internal value system.

7. They are still dependent upon the family, financially and emotionally.

8. Lasting life decisions may be made during this time.

9. They are alert to catch discrepancies between adults' behavior and the rules and values those adults express.

10. Teens have the same intense emotional needs and feelings adults have but lack understanding as to the meaning of those feelings and don't know how to cope with them.

11. Teens have a strong need to be mentored by adults whose guidance will assist them in developing personal identity.

12. When parents are absent physically or emotionally, teens feel lonely and isolated. They need parents to be present—to listen, to offer guidance, to show love and attention, to allow them to face life experiences, and to encourage independence and healthy adult-child separation.

13. Adult nurturing is needed for the teen to construct his own self-identity and develop competency.

14. If effective coping skills are not learned, teens become especially vulnerable to stressful situations.

15. If a teen feels that the family situation does not provide sufficient nurturing, he will turn to his

peer group for support.[1]

Teens of today are facing a unique set of pressures. Think with me a moment, and compare today with the time you were a teen. For example, did you have to face the possibility of a radioactive nuclear cloud circling the earth because of an atomic accident? Probably not, but today it has become a reality because of an accident at a nuclear plant in Russia. Did you have to face the threat of gang violence with two or three killings a night, every night of the week? Probably not, but in some areas of Southern California this situation is commonplace, and it is spreading to other parts of the country as well. What about AIDS? Most of us had never heard of AIDS when we were adolescents. Some of today's teens have already experienced the trauma of a friend or a family member dying from this disease.

Our present generation of teens lives under the potential of being the last generation. Even though they may not talk about it, they think about it. Wars have always been a part of life but not like today. Teens hear the same things you do through the media: threats of war, terrorist kidnappings, bombings, pollution, and social security funds running out before we reach the age of retirement. They are being raised in a promiscuous, violent, noncommittal, non-Christian society. It is a very me-centered society, and if your teen is a Christian, this in itself can create additional stress. A Christian teen is a minority person.

Moral choices are being made at an earlier age — choices about drugs, sex, friends and drinking. And to top it off, we now face the issue of AIDS and the emphasis on "safe sex."

There is another reason today's teens are more prone to difficulty in handling stress than other genera-

tions. It is not only because the rapid changes bring new pressures, but also that this generation has been given so much more in material things than previous generations have. Thus it is difficult for them to delay rewards. Instant solutions are important, and they don't know how to handle discouragement and disillusionment. As a result, they experience stress more readily, and many of them gravitate toward drugs, alcohol or even suicide.

Not all teens experience intense turmoil, but they all have their ups and down. Adolescence is one of the most difficult transitions of life. At best, it's a roller-coaster experience.

The volatile, emotional, up-and-down world of the teenager can throw parents into a turmoil. Some teens emulate a turtle and withdraw into a hard, sullen shell; others erupt like a Hawaiian volcano.

Cycle of Stress

A sequence of stressful situations where one up-setting experience leads to another can create what we call a "cycle of stress." Let's look in on a typical day in a teen's life and see how this cycle of stress develops:

1. Jerry's best friend stands him up at the donut shop before school. He then sees him driving in with a girl Jerry himself has a crush on.

2. When Jerry gets to school, he is upset and can't remember the combination for his locker. This makes him late for class and he can't hand in his assignment on time. Now he's really upset—he skipped his favorite TV show last night just so he could complete that boring assignment.

3. His teacher refuses to let him go to the office to get help with his locker, and she will not accept the late assignment.

4. As he walks back to his seat, Jerry trips over another student's pile of books in the aisle and the student swears at him and calls him a clumsy "_____."

5. Jerry swears back and threatens to punch him out. The teacher hears him but did not hear what the other student said. Jerry is given a half-hour detention.

6. The detention causes him to miss band practice.

7. Since he missed practice, he will not be allowed to go with the band and play at the Friday evening game in a neighboring town. This really infuriates him because the time on the bus with his friends is as important to Jerry as the game.

8. Upon arriving home he slams the door, cracking a window, and he snaps at his mom—who is fairly stressed out herself—and Jerry proceeds to get a lecture and a week's restriction.

Notice how one problem leads to another, and with each one Jerry seems to have less control.

A sequence of events like this, creating a cycle of stress, can happen to anyone. However, we can help our children and teens learn to interrupt the sequence and break the cycle so they can handle the problems in a much healthier manner. In this book we will look at ways to do that.

¤¤¤ **2** ¤¤¤

SOURCES OF STRESS

What is stress? Stress is any life situation that chronically bothers, irritates or upsets you. It is any type of action that places conflicting or heavy demands upon your body. What do these demands do? They simply upset the body's equilibrium.

Our bodies come equipped with a highly sophisticated defense system that helps us cope with those events in life which threaten and challenge us. When any of us feels pressured or threatened, our body quickly mobilizes its defenses for fight or flight. In the case of stress, we are infused with an abundance of adrenalin which disrupts our normal functioning and creates a heightened sense of arousal.

We are like a rubber band that is being stretched. Usually, when the pressure is released, the rubber band returns to normal. When it is stretched too much,

though, or kept in that position too long, the rubber begins to lose its elasticity, becomes brittle and develops cracks. Eventually it breaks. That is similar to what happens to us if there is too much stress in our lives.

What is stressful to one individual, however, may not be stressful to another. For some, stress is worry about future events that cannot be avoided, and then concern about the events after they have occurred. For others stress is simply the wear and tear of life. It has been called an "influential force."

Although some people think of it as tension and some as anxiety, not all stress is bad. We need a certain amount of pressure and stimulation. Stress can be good if it is short-lived. Good stress is called *"eu*stress," from the Latin word *eu,* meaning good. It is positive and helpful because it does not last, nor is it experienced continuously. The body's equilibrium soon goes back to normal. When the body does not return to normal rest and recovery, we have bad stress, or *"dis*tress."

Causes of Stress

The stress in a child or teen's life can be caused when anything happens that . . .
- —annoys him
- —threatens him
- —excites him
- —scares him
- —worries him
- —hurries him
- —frustrates him
- —angers him
- —challenges him
- —embarrasses him
- —reduces or threatens his self-esteem

Most of the time, however, it is not a particular *event* that causes stress. What then causes the problem? Most situations which produce stress involve some sort of *conflict* between ourselves and the world outside us. For example, if a teen skips school to go to the beach (which fulfills a personal desire), he creates a new problem at school with his absence. If a teen becomes over-involved at school and then has little time and energy for household responsibilities, there are new demands placed upon his family. If he doesn't balance the demands from outside with those from inside himself, he will experience stress and pressure.

Where does most of our stress come from? Whether we are children, teens or adults, it comes from our own minds. The most damaging stress comes from threats that cannot be acted upon since they exist only in our imagination. Some children and some teens imagine the worst in a situation (and so do some parents). They worry, which creates more threat and imagined fears. Even when there *is* a definite threat to the body, the problem is in the mind. Situations that worry a child can be the most troublesome of all. On the other hand, a person who has learned to live according to "Let not your heart be troubled, neither let it be afraid" (John 14:27) will be able to handle the pressures of life, both real and imagined, much better.

What kind of things do you think would cause children to experience stress? Listed on the next page are twenty situations that produce stress in a child. Which do *you* think are the most stressful? Pretend you are a child and rank these in order from 1 to 20 with 1 being the most stressful and 20 being the least.

At the end of this chapter we'll look at how the *children* rated these stress producers.

CHILDREN AND STRESS

_____ Wetting pants in class
_____ Having an operation
_____ Giving a report in class
_____ Having a scary dream
_____ Being sent to the principal's office
_____ Going blind
_____ Moving to a new school
_____ Going to the dentist
_____ Being made fun of in class
_____ Acquiring a baby sibling
_____ Being suspected of lying
_____ Being held back a year in school
_____ Not getting 100 on a test
_____ Getting lost
_____ Receiving a bad report card
_____ Losing a game
_____ Hearing parents quarrel
_____ Being caught stealing
_____ Losing a parent
_____ Being picked last for a team[1]

Other Contributors to Stress

It is important to consider several other major contributors to stress: lack of proper rest and sleep, improper diet and the "hurry disease," for instance. Putting pressure on children to perform or to hurry wires their emotions and their bodies, and it makes relaxing difficult.

Let's consider now some of the sources of that stress. For example, can you remember what bothered

you when you were in grade school? The fears, frustrations, uncertainties, pressures? Here, according to grade level, are some of the most common things that cause elementary schoolchildren to experience stress:

In *Kindergarten* the main stressors are uncertainty, fear of abandonment by an important adult, fear of wetting themselves, and fear of punishment or reprimand from their teacher.

First grade stressors are fear of riding the bus, fear of wetting in class, teacher disapproval, ridicule by peers, receiving the first report card, and fear of not passing to second grade.

In *second grade* the stressors include not understanding a certain lesson, fear of the teacher's discipline, fear of being different in some way from other children in the class, and, often, missing a particular parent.

In *third grade* stress is felt from fear of being chosen last on any team or for any activity, having to stay after school, a parent-teacher conference, fear of peer disapproval, fear of not being liked by the teacher, fear of test taking, and not enough time to finish a test or assignment.

In *fourth grade* the stressors are fear of being chosen last for anything, fear of peer disapproval of dress or appearance, fear that their friends will find new friends and share their "secrets," fear of peer ridicule, and fear of not being liked by the teacher.

In *fifth grade* the stressors are just about the same as in fourth, but there is another concern as well, that of the possibility of not being promoted and thus not being a "big sixth-grader" the next year.

In *sixth grade* there are some lingering and some

new stressors such as the fear of being chosen last for anything, peer disapproval of appearance, feeling unpopular, fear of the unknown concerning developing sexuality, and fear of not passing to junior high — as well as fear of *going* to junior high.

These are just the stressors of school. When you add to this list all the things connected to the other parts of a child's life, you discover a multitude of potential stressors,[2] and you realize that the potential for stress is all around us.

Think about the world of our children and our teens for a moment. All day they experience stimuli which can produce stress. The very state of change and flux they are in creates stress for them. Whether stress becomes a problem for them depends on how much of it they experience and how long it lasts.

To top all that off, our kids experience most of what we adults experience as well: time pressure, high expectations, divorce in the family, illness, failure, violence, jealousy, etc.

Have you ever asked your teen what he worries about regarding the future? You might want to share some of the worries you remember having when you were a teen as a way of encouraging him to open up and share with you.

The Three Stress Situations of Life

To become aware of stress in a teen's life so as to be prepared to help him, the best way to start is by identifying the three major categories of stress.

Type A Stress

The first is called *Type A* (not to be confused with the "Type A Personality") and is both *foreseeable and*

avoidable. If a teen plans to ride "The Killer" roller-coaster ride or see one of the newest blood-and-gore science-fiction movies, he knows in advance the stress he will encounter and is able to avoid it if he so desires.

There is also foreseeable and avoidable stress which is not under the teen's control. The world lives under the threat of running out of natural resources and seeing the environment become more and more polluted. Another threat is the ever-present possibility of nuclear war. Stress from these types of uncertainties is difficult for anyone to handle.

Type B Stress

Type B stress situations come from demands which are *neither foreseeable nor avoidable.* These fall into the category of crisis events such as the death of a friend or family member, an accident while in the car or while involved in sports activities, the discovery of his parents' impending divorce or separation, or learning that a sibling is gay or has AIDS.

These stressful situations place the greatest demands upon teens.

They must handle their own feelings, the situation itself, and the responses of other people as well. Both the adolescent who has to face the divorce of his parents and the teen with a torn tendon which eliminates his chances of a college sports scholarship have to adjust in two main ways: (1) thinking about themselves with a new perspective; and (2) relating to others in a different fashion.

Type C Stress

The third type of stress situation, *Type C,* is *foreseeable but not avoidable.* What kinds of situations are

foreseeable but unavoidable? Facing parents after violating curfew. Exams. Taking a three-week trip in the car with a family of five. Being drafted into the military during wartime.

Major Stresses/Problems

We know there are countless sources of stress for teens today. In 1986 an extensive survey was conducted by *Children and Teens Today*. The readership of this magazine has a common element—whether they are ministers, lay counselors, therapists, administrators or counselors, they all work directly with children and/or adolescents.

The question was: What do you see as the major stresses/problems facing today's teenagers? Of eight suggested answers given, 72.4 percent of those who responded listed "problems arising from parental divorce/remarriage," with "peer pressure to drink/alcoholism" coming in second at 68.2 percent. Here is how people pinpointed the remaining six problems listed:

59%–acceptance of sexual intercourse/experimentation at a young age;

48%–pressure to experiment with drugs;

45%–depression;

30%–the need to attain academic excellence;

28%–attempts at suicide;

23%–fears arising from the threat of nuclear war.

The readers were invited to describe other major problems which were not listed, and the problems mentioned most often were parent and family-related difficulties.[3]

Let's look at an adult stress study and apply it to the lives of children and teens. The Holmes-Rahe Life

X

Event Scale[4] serves as our example.

You will find below the forty-three life events listed in that scale. They have been adjusted to fit situations in the life of a child—that is, "spouse" is changed to "parent," "work" to "school," etc. The point value of each life event remains the same.

LIFE EVENTS

1. Death of a parent 100
2. Divorce of parents 73
3. Separation of parents 65
4. Parent's jail term 63
5. Death of a close family member (e.g., a grandparent) 63
6. Personal injury or illness 53
7. Parent's remarriage 50
8. Suspension or expulsion from school 47
9. Parents' reconciliation 45
10. Long vacation (Christmas, summer, etc.) . . . 45
11. Parent's or sibling's sickness 44
12. Mother's pregnancy 40
13. Anxiety over sex 39
14. Birth of new baby (or adoption) 39
15. New school, classroom or teacher 39
16. Money problems at home 38
17. Death (or moving away) of close friend 37
18. Change in studies 36
19. More quarrels with parents 36
20. (Not applicable to a child or teen)
21. (Not applicable to a child or teen)

Totaling the score, you may be surprised to find how quickly an average child can reach the 300-point level of severe stress potential. Changes occur rapidly in a child's life, far more rapidly than in the life of his parents. Six hours of school alone can subject him to the possibility of any combination of life events 8, 10, 15, 18, 22, 25, 27, 31 or 43 on almost a routine basis. In addition, the ups and downs of his social life add the chance of stress from life events 13, 17, 32, 36, 39, or 41. He is especially susceptible to personal injury because of the high percentage of his time spent in physical activities such as bike riding or skating. In addition, he may fall victim to any contagious disease that strikes the school.

We as parents cannot eliminate all the stresses of a child's life. Some of them will always be there, but we can do the following:

1. Realize that our children live under constant stress.
2. Recognize any stressors that we or our environment tend to place on a child.
3. Take steps to eliminate those stressors which can be eliminated.
4. Teach our children how to handle the stressors of life.[5]

On the next page are the stress-producing situations listed on page 22 in the order in which the children perceived them, from most stressful to least stressful.

KIDS' RESPONSES TO CHILDREN AND STRESS

1. Losing a parent
2. Going blind
3. Being held back a year in school
4. Wetting pants in school
5. Hearing parents quarrel
6. Being caught stealing
7. Being suspected of lying
8. Receiving a bad report card
9. Being sent to the principal's office
10. Having an operation
11. Getting lost
12. Being made fun of in class
13. Moving to a new school
14. Having a scary dream
15. Not getting 100 on a test
16. Being picked last for a team
17. Losing in a game
18. Going to the dentist
19. Giving a report in class
20. Acquiring a baby sibling[6]

Compare your answers with those of the children here. How close did you come? If you are like most parents, you will be surprised by the results. Does this make you want to listen more closely to your children?

Why not ask your own children to rank these in the same way for themselves? You may be surprised.

¤¤¤ 3 ¤¤¤

SYMPTOMS OF STRESS

Each and every day we face the possibility of stress. As adults we just accept that we will encounter pressure and tension in our lives. However, we sometimes fail to realize that a child can be stressed every bit as much or even more than we are. After all, we have lived longer and have developed some coping skills. A young child is still in the formative stages of his or her life. He doesn't have the coping ability that we do, and when a child is stressed, he will show it in one way or another.

Symptoms of Stress in Your Young Child

You may be asking, "How do I know if my child is under a lot of stress?"

There are many symptoms. If these symptoms occur frequently and persistently, listen to the message that's being given to you.

Some of the symptoms are:

— chronic irritability
— difficulty concentrating
— difficulty sleeping or difficulty staying awake
— poor eating habits such as impulsive, uncontrolled eating
— restlessness
— rapid heart rate
— backaches
— neckaches
— headaches
— muscles aching for no apparent reason
— irritating behavior
— lack of spontaneity
— frequent mood shifts
— nervous habits such as twitches, nail biting, pulling at hair, biting lips

If you notice these signs, especially a combination of them, you can be fairly sure your child needs help to learn to respond to life in a healthier manner

Teaching Your Child to Spot Stress

Childhood is a long time of life, a time of preparation, growth and development. During this period, children face some of the same stressors as adults, but without the same resources. You can help your child by explaining what stress is and teaching him how to recognize it when it occurs. You can help him monitor his own life. This can be done best by helping the child recognize the symptoms of stress.

If your child came to you and asked, "What is stress? How do I know when I have it?" what would you

say? How would you describe stress to a child?

Perhaps you could say, "Stress can result from what happens between people. Your friend may be mad at you, or the students in class may have made fun of you and it really hurt. It can occur when you don't get enough sleep or when there is too much going on. In addition, you can cause your own stress by what you think about yourself. If you think you're dumb or no good or not pretty, those ideas can cause stress."

In explaining what stress is to your child, you may want to use this "Have you ever . . . ?" approach:

Have you ever had your heart beat faster?
Have you ever had your hands get cold and
   sweaty?
Have you ever had your stomach get in a
   knot?
Have you ever had your tummy hurt?
Have you ever gotten nervous?
Have you ever felt sad or giggled a lot?
Have you ever felt mean, or like crying, or
   that you wanted to get back at someone?
Have you ever had frightening dreams?
Have you ever not been able to concentrate?
Have you ever been grouchy?
Have you ever not gotten along with other
   people?
(And any other questions you can think of.)

If a child understands that these symptoms could be caused by stress, it can help him monitor his own life and be able to put to use some of the stress reduction suggestions given later in this book.

Spotting Stress in Your Teen

Teens face stressful situations continually. If a peer group uses drugs or alcohol, for example, or engages in petty theft, the people in the group will pressure your teen to participate. Yet he knows that the consequences will create additional pressure through the response of parents, church leaders and teachers, and according to his own value system.

The one issue which affects a teen's response to stress more often than all others is the development of his own identity.

Instability of emotional expression is a normal characteristic of this turbulent quest, and the state of an adolescent's identity fluctuates continually.

The teen's identity starts to develop as he begins to withdraw from his parents. He becomes a "separate" person by rejecting customary family patterns.

This is the time he begins to determine what is important to him, establish his own value system, and develop his own unique personality and identity.

A teen doesn't have to have a certain type of personality in order to have a solid identity. Some are outgoing and some are introverted. Some are factually oriented and some are quite emotional in their response to life.

In order to recognize when your teen shows signs of reacting to stress, it will help if you understand the two basic types of teenage identities, the *integrated* and the *non-integrated*. The integrated identity is one in which attitudes, values and abilities are connected with one another in a harmonious manner. The non-integrated identity is built upon a set of attitudes, values and habits which are more or less unconnected and

could be in conflict. Teens with non-integrated identities often feel they have to choose between looking out for themselves and giving in to others. They mismanage stress because their inner conflicts create inner stress and make it difficult for them to respond in a positive manner to the outward situations.

Reactions to Type A Situations

In a Type A stress situation, the non-integrated teen will usually be either an anxious teen or a conforming teen. The anxious teen, when confronted with a foreseeable but avoidable problem, will worry and stew over his decision. He has difficulty deciding whether to give in or try to avoid the situation. He may instead come up with an alternative: He may get sick. Headaches, psychosomatic symptoms, fatigue, boredom and stomach aches are common. Because of low self-esteem and a disconnected set of values and attitudes, this teen tends to avoid the stressful situation in a self-punishing manner.

With the other non-integrated response, which is to conform, the teen is looking for a "quick-fix" to alleviate the stress while at the same time gaining peer group approval and acceptance. Remember, the peer group's influence is the most powerful on the teen who has this non-integrated identity. He lacks the inner strength to resist conforming. He wants to grow up and become independent, but does not know how. However, conforming brings about its own set of problems and stresses which the teen does not think about and which continue to compound the problem.

Reactions to Type B Situations

Type B situations, those which are both unforeseeable and unavoidable, are difficult not only for

teens, but for adults as well. They are often very intense, and they tend to disrupt our life plans. For teens, these can be devastating since they undermine an already fragile sense of self-esteem.

People react in a number of different ways when hit by a crisis. Integrated teens, those who cope well in a Type B crisis situation, are those who:

- have another person who stands by them and gives support;
- understand the meaning of what they have lost in the crisis;
- are able to handle their own feelings of guilt;
- have a reason to live—they have hope;
- have a biblical perspective on life (these teens respond the best).

(For additional information, see the chapter entitled "The Questions of Life" in *How to Have a Creative Crisis* by this author.[1])

It is actually possible to predict which teens will have the most difficulty in a Type B situation. Those with a non-integrated personality can be overwhelmed in a crisis because they are emotionally weak. They often respond in ways that make the problem worse.

If they are physically ailing, they do not have the best resources with which to respond.

If they deny the problem or tend to deny reality most of the time, they struggle with understanding and acceptance.

If they have the tendency to talk, eat or drink excessively, they tend to exaggerate those behaviors and make matters worse.

If they are impulsive and have to have problems fixed "immediately," or if they tend to procrastinate, the problem becomes greater.

Blamers have a hard time coping with a crisis. They ask, "Who caused the problem?" rather than asking, "What's the solution?"

Those who are overly dependent cling to others and those who are independent avoid any assistance. Each of these reactions feeds the problem.

Type B situations are viewed not as events which could happen to any teen but as difficulties specifically directed toward them, either because of bad luck or because that's the way life is! Some teens feel they are the only ones to have these problems, and they tend to become self-punishers. They behave in a manner that pushes others away, and they tend not to trust anyone — other teens or adults.

Another response is that of competition and challenge. Some teens feel they can change their luck so they challenge the problem without adequate planning or anticipation of the consequences. They could become addicted to the challenge, and they could even cheat or steal in order to resolve the problem.

Reactions to Type C Stress Situations

In the Type C stress situation, which is foreseeable but not avoidable, a common reaction is anger. Going to the dentist, taking an exam, or having to take a vacation with abusive parents — each falls into the Type C category. It could include doing chores or homework. Many teens have difficulty with these situations and often make it miserable for others around them.

Each situation becomes a war zone over power

and control. Everything involves a struggle and the teen usually has an excuse. He projects blame onto other people or events. If you're the parent of such a teen, don't be surprised if you feel a great deal of anger yourself. These teens have the ability to provoke this response. Their display of cool control and arrogance is a cover-up for their inner feelings of fragmentation.

Other teens, however, respond with a great deal of fear. Some develop phobias about school. Teens who live in homes where there is physical abuse, substance abuse, or continual rejection are often fearful. A frightened teen looks to others for solutions to his problems and often will do almost anything if someone accepts him and is kind to him.

Teens' Coping Techniques

A common coping technique is to run away from home. It is estimated that approximately one million teens run away each year. These teens are open to exploitation. They don't blame others, though; they blame themselves.

Often a teen responds with behavior that has a hidden message. For example, self-mutilating teens, through their deliberate and radical behavior, express their independence. This behavior also can be their way of trying to control their fears, sexual thoughts, or violent and aggressive impulses. In talking to a teen, you may hear him say, "It's my body and I will do with it what I want, and nobody can stop me. Just try. It won't work." Any efforts to control their outward behavior without dealing with their inner feelings will be ineffective.

Alienation and personality restriction is another means of expressing depression and stress. Many older

teens feel apathetic and out of touch with themselves and others, which results in inaction. The teen avoids anything that might lead to a failure and any aspiration that could bring disappointment. He will not expose himself to any heartache. He is not a risk taker.

Sometimes a teen will unwittingly adopt a particular role in order to handle the stresses in his life. Let's consider some of these roles in light of what the teen is trying to accomplish.

Some teens are *dreamers*. This often happens when they are bored. They dream about how life could be better, or they begin to imagine a new type of life. Do you know what your teen's daydreams are? Have you ever shared some of your own that you had when you were a teen, or even now? Talking about your own dreams may open the door for you to discover your teen's fantasies as well.

Some teens are *complainers*. They collect grievances, and they gripe and complain about friends, teachers, parents, school, and anything that walks in front of them. Making something or someone else look bad makes them feel better. They lessen their stress feelings by blaming others.

Other teens are *brooders*. They say very little outwardly, but a great deal goes on inside their minds. They often focus on how unfair life is.

The *joker* reacts in the opposite way. He doesn't seem to take life seriously at all. This is often a mask hiding the teen's insecurity and fear of getting close to others. The humor is used to avoid intimacy and also to gain attention and recognition.

Some teens are *charmers*. They know how to manipulate others and often act years younger than

they are. It seems to work for them. Though they are charming, they appear to be somewhat incapable and dependent. This is their way of coping.

Have you ever come across the *excuse maker?* If he's late, it's someone else's fault. To handle stress, he gives an excuse. He avoids the pain of personal responsibility. This is his way of lessening his own stress.

Other teens become *escape artists* in an effort to avoid their problems. They escape into school activities, their church, hobbies, sports, etc., but they never get around to resolving the situation that is creating the stress.

Some become *actors* to handle their stress. They deny their pain or loss or that they are upset, and they seem to get on with their lives. Unfortunately, we often tend to encourage their denials by saying, "How well you are handling that upsetting situation!"

These non-integrated teens need a lot of help. Often they will need more help than we as parents can provide. The help could include support groups, counseling or even family therapy. Without help, these teens will get worse before they get better — and getting better does not usually happen naturally.

The non-integrated teen is unable to avoid, cope with, or prepare for stress. To make matters worse, he tends to create and expose himself to more stress — which turns into a vicious cycle. Because of the additional stress he experiences and creates, he has to spend more time and emotional energy trying to cope, and that leaves less of those two vital elements for healthy growth. Each of his teen years, then, brings additional stress, which he is less and less capable of handling.[2]

Stress Overload

What are the major symptoms of stress overload? There are a number of signals that make this easy to detect. Which of these symptoms are evident in your teen?

_____ Difficulties in making both major and minor decisions.

_____ Excessive daydreaming or fantasizing about "getting away from it all."

_____ Increased use of cigarettes, alcohol, stimulants or tranquilizers.

_____ Thoughts trailing off while speaking or writing. The person wonders, *What am I saying?* and can't understand why he loses his train of thought.

_____ Excessive worrying about all areas of life; taking on almost everyone else's worries in addition to his own.

_____ Sudden outbursts of temper and hostility.

_____ Paranoid ideas and mistrust of friends and family.

_____ Forgetfulness of appointments, deadlines and dates.

_____ Frequent spells of brooding and feelings of inadequacy.

_____ Reversals in usual behavior. People say, "He acts like a different person."[3]

Recognizing the symptoms is a big step toward identifying the problems and can point you in the right direction to find and implement possible solutions.

On the other hand, some teens are able to face their problems themselves. They have the ability to confront their difficulties and to find ways to resolve them. Many teens are able to do this because of the

inner faith they have in Jesus Christ and because they have learned to rely on God. They have discovered that their strength and stability come from being dependent on Him.

¤¤¤ 4 ¤¤¤

IDENTIFYING THE PROBLEMS

As we noted in the last chapter, one of the biggest sources of upset for a child, especially a teen, is the development of his identity. Yet everyone has to go through it in order to reach adulthood. Dr. Keith Olson says it is necessary for a person to "develop a sense of personal identity that consistently establishes who he is as an integrated individual throughout each life role, separate and different from every other person."[1]

If a child has a healthy identity and a good sense of self-esteem, he will be better able to evaluate the risk of not giving in to outside pressures. The momentary satisfaction of peer group approval is not nearly as important as his lasting sense of self-respect. A person must learn to say no to his peers and handle the pressure he receives from them in return. Our goal as parents and teachers is to help our children and our

teens develop a strong sense of positive identity and help them anticipate the pressures that will be exerted by their peer group and know how to respond to them.

As a child reaches his teen years, he begins to venture out from the family shores, but in such a way that he does not completely sever his family ties and support. This is a bit like walking a tightrope for the parents. Their main task at this time is to start relinquishing control, bit by bit, the right amount at the right time, as the teen spends more time with his peers and less with his parents. A balance of freedom and parental control is necessary if the teen is to learn through experience how to handle stress.

Eventually a teen pushes off completely from the safe shoreline of his parents and paddles for several years through turbulent waters of maturing until he reaches the theoretically "calmer" shores of adulthood. Teens experience many crises during these transitional years, and their efforts to find and be themselves sometimes give rise to intense frustrations.

Why do some teenagers seem to handle the transition of adolescence so well while others seem to be stress-prone, going straight from one stressful situation to another? Can we in some way identify these stress-prone individuals? Yes, there is a way. Everyone has the potential to be overwhelmed by stress, but some have greater difficulty than others with the pressures of life.

One type of stress-prone teen, or younger child, is very obvious. Perhaps you know one like this. He (or she) is always in a hurry, has to be the best, tends to take on too much for himself, often interrupts or over-reacts to others, and has difficulty losing. The number of students who manifest these characteristics seems to be greater in suburban schools than in rural ones. That

could be because of the intense competitiveness among those whose upper-middle-class parents have chosen to make their homes in the suburbs.

These pressured kids tend to compete excessively for grades. I've even seen some who are not satisfied unless they receive the top *A* in the class. They are over-ambitious and have great difficulty handling disappointments. You won't find them having an easy time relaxing. They over-involve themselves in whatever they do, and when a goal is attained, they quickly search for another. Participation in and of itself is not sufficient. They must also achieve recognition.

These children and young people are well on the way to becoming classic Type A adults. This tendency doesn't usually begin in adulthood — it begins in childhood and becomes more evident during the teen years. This type of personality carries with it the possibility of a premature heart attack.

Another way to identify the person who has difficulty with stress but whose symptoms are not quite so obvious is by using an adaptation of the "Capable Kid Test" below. This test originally was designed for children but I feel it can be applied to teens as well. Identifying a child or teen's attitude and noting his comments regarding stressful situations will tell you much about his state.

THE CAPABLE KID TEST

Step 1. Think of a situation that your child or teen has experienced as stressful. It could be sharing a room or the car with a sibling, having a favorite weekend or a date cancelled, flunking a test, not making the school team or play, being shunned by friends, being embarrassed, etc.

Step 2. Think about how he reacted and whether that is his typical response to that type of situation.

Step 3. Choose **one** statement from the following list that best describes his reactions. (Select the first one that strikes you as appropriate.)

1. "Things like this always happen to me."
2. He becomes unreasonably quiet and walks away.
3. "I never get what I want. Nobody cares about me." (May become belligerent and verbally abusive.)
4. "Boy, am I disappointed." Then a few seconds later, "Oh, well, maybe it will work out the next time."
5. "This is no surprise. I was expecting something cruddy like this to happen." (Then becomes withdrawn and preoccupied.)
6. "That sure makes me angry, but I didn't know. Is there anything I can do about it now?"
7. "That is not fair. It's just not fair!" (And proceeds to have a child's or adolescent's temper tantrum.)
8. Doesn't visibly react, but just withdraws. He won't talk about it and tends to isolate himself.

Step 4. Now, find the description of your child or teen as indicated below. (Remember, the description you select should be his typical way of responding.) This will clarify for you the level of ability your child or teen has to handle stress.

#4 or #6—Either of these responses indicate a capable person. He handles stress well. This person will express his disappointment or anger and then quickly figure out what to do about it. He will be disappointed rather than greatly upset, and it will last for

only a few minutes.

#1, #2 or #7—This is a slightly vulnerable child or teen. He has upset reactions, but they don't last long. He soon calms down, becomes less preoccupied with himself, and begins to make statements about how he can handle the problem. He could learn some new ways of coping so he wouldn't be so reactive.

#3, #5 or #8—This person is seriously vulnerable. His response usually lasts more than twenty-four hours, and symptoms of being vulnerable are evident in his life.[2]

Here are some of the most important characteristics of the capable child (or teen) and the vulnerable one:

The Capable Child
- resourceful
- confident
- able to confront people or situations when concerned or upset about something
- willing to take risks
- relaxed
- responsible
- able to express feelings easily
- endowed with a sense of direction

The Vulnerable Child
- withdrawn, preoccupied
- often sick without an organic cause
- isolated
- secretive, noncommunicative
- belligerent, uncooperative
- overly sensitive
- in need of excessive reassurance

Identifying Sources of Stress in Your Child or Teen

Whenever you observe the symptoms of stress in your child, you need to identify the source. Look for its beginnings. You may want to ask yourself some of the following questions:

- Where is the source of this stress? Is it within the family (such as Dad taking a new job which requires frequent absences)? Or is it outside the family (perhaps failing a major math test)?

- Does the stress affect all the family members (as with a death), or just the child (having a close friend move away) or teen (a breakup with a romantic interest)?

- Was this stressful experience sudden (an accident or illness) or did it come on gradually (observing a close friend get sick and then die or watching a close friend become addicted)?

- What is the degree of the stress? Is it intense (a death of someone close) or mild (a cold which causes the child to miss a ball game)?

- Does this stressor require a short-term adjustment (arguing with a friend) or is it long-term (mononucleosis)?

- Was the situation expected (knowing a close friend is moving) or was it unexpected and unpredictable (a fire in the home)?

- Do the family members feel the stressor is one which can be adjusted to fairly soon (going to a new school) or is it beyond anyone's control (terminally ill parent with no prospects in sight for improvement)?

You will be enabled to help your child on a more long-term basis as you continue to be aware of every stressful situation. Each one carries with it both pain and potential for growth.

Identifying Stressors Peculiar to Teens

What creates stress for teens? If you can identify the sources of stress in your teen's life, you can help him learn to handle some of his stress-potential situations, and he will be better equipped then to handle other crises he may face as he approaches maturity.

Several factors that can bring about stress apply particularly to teens. I encourage you to look for any of these conditions in your teen's life:

1. *Boredom or lack of meaning.* That this leads to stress may sound strange, yet many teens do not find a challenge or meaning for their existence. This is an opportunity for you to help your teen discover the meaning that Christ gives to life. Helping a teen see life through God's perspective can bring meaning no matter what the teen is doing or what is happening to him.

2. *Time pressures and deadlines.* The stress these create is often of our own doing. Some children today are growing up hurried, and this continues into adulthood. What they see on television, in movies and from advertisers hurries them along the road toward being "grown up" before they can handle it emotionally.

3. *An excessive workload.* The pressure this creates is many times self-induced. Many teens will take on too many activities and be involved in too many things at one time.

4. *Unrealistic expectations* of oneself or of another person (e.g., teacher or parent). This can lead to

dissatisfaction. Suggest to your teen that he do the following:

a. List the expectations he thinks his parents have of him.

b. Itemize each of his expectations of himself.

c. Identify where each came from.

d. Think about and answer this question: "Why are these expectations important and how would my life be affected if they were not met?"

5. *Role conflicts.* Teens may be involved in activities or classes that do not fit their gifts, capabilities or interests, and they may feel stuck—and this creates tension.

6. *School environment.* A monotonous and repetitious environment can be just as much a problem as a fast-paced, pressure-filled, competitive atmosphere. School can be very stressful. Having six to eight classes a day with different teachers and a different set of peers in each class can be disruptive. Having a report due, or a test scheduled, the same week in each class can be stressful. If the curriculum is too demanding or too boring and unchallenging for the teen's level of ability, this too can be stressful. If the teen does not understand an assignment and there is little help available from the teacher, the pressure and frustration can build.

7. *Lack of communication in a relationship.* When open communication and an open show of emotions are blocked, it is not only stressful but also discouraging and can lead to depression in the life of a person who already has low self-esteem. If a teen has uncertainties about his relationship with a friend or with his parents, stress could be

present.

8. *A performance-based self-esteem.* Those who build their sense of identity and self-esteem upon an inadequate basis such as work, appearance, grades or athletic ability will experience a great deal of pressure and tension.

9. *The Type A personality.* This becomes a major cause of stress for the teen himself as well as for other family members and for fellow workers. The tendency starts in childhood and many teens are prone to be overly influenced by this "hurry-up" pressure.

10. *Loud and excessively rhythmic music.* What does music mean to a teen? It may be an expression of uniqueness, rebellion or peer group involvement. For some teens it is a way to assert independence and power.[3] Neither teens nor adults, however, realize how much stress is produced by the "noise" many teens call music. Unfortunately, many parents take the attitude, "Oh, well, that's just a phase he's going through. It's loud and unintelligible, but I guess it's not all that bad."

Isn't it? Let's consider the effect of music.

Some music can stimulate romantic feelings; other music can create a feeling of sadness or depression. Some music peps us up and makes us move faster. Researchers have proven that our bodies respond to sounds whether the sound registers consciously or unconsciously.

Radionics is the study of the effect of vibrations on the health and strength of the body. It focuses especially on how muscles and organs respond to sound.

Did you know that musical rhythms physically affect your teen's brain and heart? Did you know that both hard and soft rock create physiological and psychological tension and can disrupt the inner rhythm of the body? And that disco music, with its mix of instruments and volume, produces stress on the body? Insistent rhythms can arouse agitated feelings which include tension, excitement and even sexual arousal.

Too much sound can lead to annoyance, frustration and distraction—stress that can lower the quality of a person's emotional life. According to former Surgeon General of the United States Dr. William H. Stewart, too much continual noise can create adverse physiological changes in the body's cardiovascular, glandular and respiratory system. It can also cause stress on the muscular responses.

You have the right, for your own sanity's sake and to maintain control of your own stress level as well as to help your teen, to exercise control over the volume of the music, what is played, and when it is played.

Effects of Stress on Others

You should be aware of the fact that others in the family are always affected when any member experiences stress. Stress does not usually become evident in just one person. The situation which causes the stress for that person nearly always causes stress, although at various levels, for others in the home as well.

The following activity will help you evaluate stress levels among the various members of your family. Let me suggest that you ask each person to complete

this evaluation, and then share your responses with one another.

STRESS EVALUATION

1. When have you experienced the greatest amount of stress during the last five years? What contributed to this stress?

Time	Cause	Who did you share this with?
Present to 1 year ago		
1-2 years ago		
2-3 years ago		
3-4 years ago		
4-5 years ago		

2. During the last five years, which family member do you think has experienced the greatest amount of stress, and what contributed to that stress?

Time	Cause	Who did the person share this with?
Present to 1 year ago		
1-2 years ago		
2-3 years ago		
3-4 years ago		
4-5 years ago		

3. Indicate which, if any, of these possible circumstances or conditions could cause stress for you:

_____ Boredom or lack of memory

_____ Time pressures and deadlines

_____ Excessive workload

_____ Unrealistic expectations

_____ Perfectionism

_____ Role conflicts

_____ Blocked emotions

_____ Environment

_____ Concern over a relationship

_____ Inflexibility

_____ Identity and self-esteem built upon an
        inadequate basis

_____ Type A personality tendencies

_____ Music and noise

As stress in the entire family is identified, dealt with and reduced, the stressed teen will benefit in several ways—through direct changes in his own life as well as through adjustments in his environment. Healthier and happier family relationships can be a transformation welcomed by everyone in the home.

¤¤¤ **5** ¤¤¤

FEARS

One way to understand the stressors of children is to understand their fears. Why? Because so much childhood stress stems from fear.

How do we recognize a child's fears? What indicates that anxiety is present?

Some children are quite verbal about their fears and you have little difficulty being aware. Others either avoid thinking about them or make it a point not to share them. However, whether he talks about it openly or not, if a child is fearful or troubled with anxiety, you probably will notice some of the following symptoms.

Symptoms of Fear

Children who have difficulty concentrating and who become either listless or hyperactive may be struggling with inner anxiety. They could be experiencing

stress. If their appetite changes from eating very little to consuming greater amounts of food, this too could be a sign of anxiety. Bedwetting, nightmares, restlessness, insomnia, unusual talkativeness, stuttering, panic attacks, compulsive behaviors or obsessive thought patterns are additional indications of fear. Often a wide range of bodily complaints will be the indication of fear, or it may accompany any of the above.

One grandmother said to me, "I can always tell how my daughter and son-in-law are getting along by how much my granddaughter is stuttering."

Some Specific Basic Fears

Let's look at some of the basic fears of childhood as suggested by Erik Erikson (who has pioneered studies in the developmental stages of life).

Children fear **withdrawal of support**. This pressure can be felt both at home and at school, and children fear the withdrawal of peers as well as that of adults. Being too smart or not smart enough can turn peers away. Wearing the wrong clothes can have the same effect!

QUESTIONS (to ask your child): What kind of help do you like? How do you feel when someone takes it away? How can you handle this?

Children fear **suddenness**. Infants respond to sudden movements around them with a startled response. This continues throughout childhood. Adults may plan deliberately for some time to make major moves such as taking a new job and moving into a new home in another state, but for the child, it doesn't become a reality until it happens. This is true even if it has been discussed with him before. He needs much talk and anticipatory planning.

QUESTIONS: What kind of sudden, unexpected things frighten you most? How can we learn to handle these?

Fear of **noise** takes its toll on children, even infants, and we live in a noisy world. Four-month-old Lee became visibly agitated when his mother set a wound-up music box down beside him and turned it on. She had to take it away.

QUESTIONS: What noises bother you the most? How can you learn to handle noise?

Fear of **interruption** can be a real frustration to a child. A child's concentration on an activity can be intense, but an adult often will interrupt since, from the adult's perspective, that activity isn't important. However, playing, reading, talking, watching TV, or even just sitting around — any of these can be extremely meaningful activities for a child.

QUESTIONS: What interruptions bother you most? How can you handle those that can't be avoided?

Children fear **having something important to them taken away**. If you are a parent, you already know how possessive children feel about "their" things. These can be tangible things such as a rock collection, or they can be something intangible such as being the best student in the class. The child fears losing either.

QUESTIONS: What are you most afraid of losing? How can you handle losing something?

You know that children are afraid of too much restraint, but do you know they also fear **too much freedom**? Children do not like to be tied down to too many rules or restrictions, but an overabundance of freedom gives them more independence than they can

handle. A balance is needed between parents and schools being restrictive and permissive.

QUESTIONS: What kinds of restrictions or rules bother you the most? What are the times you wish there were more rules or restrictions? What can you do when there are too many or not enough rules? How can you learn to handle this?

Children fear **being exposed**. In school, one question many children dread hearing is the one that comes when a test paper has been returned and the child has seen his bad grade—his friend turns around and asks, "What did you get?" Children feel exposed when they try for the honor roll and don't make it. Some children experience exposure when their parents listen in on their private conversations on the phone—these children learn to be secretive.

QUESTIONS: How do you feel when someone finds out something about you that you don't want them to know? What could you say or do to handle that better?

Strange as it seems, many children fear **being small** or remaining small. One of the status symbols in our society is bigness. Big houses, big athletes, big babies—all are given notice. In school, older students appear so large to a child that his own shortness is magnified. Boys are concerned about the size of their penis and girls want to be the first in their group to wear a bra. What does a child feel when others call him or her "Shorty"?

QUESTIONS: How do you feel about your size? What size do you want to become? What will you do if you end up smaller than that?

A fear common to both adults and children is

being left alone. Girls, especially, feel this fear, which accounts for the strong cliques preteen girls form.

Separation from mother is one of a child's greatest fears. Unfortunately, we live in a society where children are separated from their parents a great deal — because of divorce, both parents working, too many outside activities, pressures at home, or neglect. In school, children are upset when a favorite teacher leaves or when they are punished by being isolated from the rest of the class.

QUESTIONS: How do you feel when you are left alone? When might you be afraid of being alone? What does it feel like to be lonely? What can you do to handle the lonely times?

More Fears

In addition to those listed above, here are two more common childhood fears, along with some suggestions as to what can be done about them.

For many children an **animal** is an object of fear. (It is for many adults as well.) How do you help a child who is afraid of an animal? One thing you *don't* do is force the child to face the fear all at once, for he does not have the resources to cope with it.

Let's assume that a child is afraid of cats. A cat may appear small to us, but look at it from the child's point of view. A thirty-pound child looking at a ten- or fifteen-pound cat sees something very different from what you and I see. If you can imagine a cat that is half or a third of your weight, your response might be a bit more cautious. Also, even though cats look harmless, their claws are sharp. Cats sometimes bite, and they are unpredictable. How do you then help a child? (The following approach can be used with a number of other

animals or fear objects as well.)

Instead of pushing the child toward his total fear, try gradual exposure. Show him pictures of a cat or point out the qualities of cats on the various ads on television. Let the child watch you demonstrate your joy in handling a cat. Let the child know that he can pet the cat as you do. Don't force him to do so, but when he does touch the cat, talk about how soft the cat's fur is, how pretty it is, etc. It is important to select a cat that is calm and one that responds positively to love and attention. Encourage the child to pet the cat with you more and more frequently. The time will come when the child is able to do this on his own and be spontaneous about it.

Some parents have found it helpful to have the child keep a written record of his progress regarding whatever it is that he fears or that upsets his life. Such a written record shows the child he is attaining a goal. For example, the record might indicate when the child responded to a cat, how long, where, and what his positive feelings were.

In addition to the fear of animals, **nighttime** fears—such as fear of the **dark** and of **nightmares**— are very common.

Darkness can be especially frightening to a child, for it generates a sense of feeling isolated, abandoned or lost. A gradual approach once again can be helpful. A child needs to know that it is all right to talk about his fears, that he will not be made fun of for being afraid. You might try gradually reducing the amount of light in the child's room. Share the following verse with the child and help him commit it to memory:

When you lie down you shall not be afraid; yes, you shall lie down and your sleep shall be sweet. Be not

afraid of sudden terror and panic, nor of the stormy
blast or the storm and ruin of the wicked when it
comes [for you will be guiltless], for the Lord shall
be your confidence, firm and strong, and shall keep
your foot from being caught [in a trap or hidden
danger] (Proverbs 3:24-26, *The Amplified Bible*).

Many children have nightmares or, as they call
them, "bad dreams," three to six times a month. When
you or I take a fear to bed with us it often crops up again
in our dreams — our minds run wild during our sleep.
So we realize that children's persistent and repetitive
nightmares may indicate that excessive tension, stress
or fear has been felt during their day. When their
dreams occur nightly or several times a night, it may be
telling you something. (For specific and detailed help
with children's fears, see *Helping the Fearful Child*, by
Dr. Jonathan Kellerman.[1])

To understand your child's fears and anxieties
better, ask him what he thinks about when he is going
to sleep at night. Ask him if he's ever afraid or if he ever
worries. Read him the following poem and see how he
responds.

WHATIF

Last night, while I lay thinking here,
Some Whatifs crawled inside my ear
And pranced and partied all night long
And sang their same old Whatif song:
Whatif I'm dumb in school?
Whatif they've closed the swimming pool?
Whatif I get beat up?
Whatif there's poison in my cup?
Whatif I flunk that test?
Whatif green hair grows on my chest?

Whatif nobody likes me?
Whatif a bolt of lightning strikes me?
Whatif I don't grow taller?
Whatif my head starts getting smaller?
Whatif the wind tears up my kite?
Whatif they start a war?
Whatif my parents get divorced?
Whatif the bus is late?
Whatif my teeth don't grow in straight?
Whatif I tear my pants?
Whatif I never learn to dance?
Everything seems swell, and then
The nighttime Whatifs strike again!

(Source unknown)

You might want to share with your child some of the worries you can remember having when you were young as a way to encourage your child to share his with you. You could make a game of it. Read a list of your own "whatifs" to your child and then ask your child what his "whatifs" are.

How We Can Help

Children learn most of their fears. This means that it is also possible for them to unlearn them. Dr. Kellerman suggests a number of practical and workable ways to help children rid their lives of fear:

1. Let the child know that *it is all right to be afraid*. Everyone has fears at some time in his life. A certain amount of fear is normal and we don't have to be ashamed when we are afraid. Share your own childhood fears and let the child know those fears passed from your life. This can be an encouragement to him.

2. Help the child understand that *being afraid*

is temporary. He may even fear that his fear will last forever. Children need a message of hope for the future.

3. Let the child know that *it is good to talk about his fear.* Sharing it helps him keep it in perspective and avoid distortions. His sharing will help you to know the extent of his fear, and then you are better equipped to help him overcome any distortions. Many parents have found it easier for the child when they have him draw his feelings or fears on a piece of paper with crayons, or act out his fantasies, or use puppets to talk out his fears.

4. Let the child know that *it is also normal not to be afraid.* When a child can observe another person not being afraid in a situation where he is fearful, he gets the message that it is possible not to be afraid.

5. Help the child learn that *a new behavior will replace his fear response.* These new responses are called counter behaviors or fear-replacing behaviors. Encourage the child to imagine himself not being afraid in his usual fear experience. These kinds of positive imageries are powerful substitutes which we could all use to greater effectiveness. Even encouraging a child to become angry in his fear situation can be beneficial. It is difficult to be both fearful and angry at the same time. The anger will give him a greater feeling of control. Participating in a positive activity or favorite pastime when the feared object or situation is at hand can eventually lessen the fear.

As with adults, so with children—repeated facing of a fear is the best method of overcoming it. We all need to use the creative powers of our God-given imagination to visualize ourselves handling the fearful event. Depending upon the comprehension level of the child, selected portions of Scripture will help bring

peace and comfort to his mind.

One of the underlying themes of fear for both children and adults is the fear of the unknown. We desire certainty. We want to be assured that we will be all right, that we will be safe, that our questions will be answered, and that we will be able to do what we are asked to do.

Many of our other specific fears have their roots in this fear. However, though we may not know all that will happen, God does know. The psalmist says, "Thou knowest my downsitting and mine uprising, thou understandest my thought afar off" (Psalm 139:2, KJV).

One of the great lessons of life for a child is to come to the place where he can say, "It's all right for me not to know all the answers because I trust in God and He helps me handle life's uncertainties."

¤ ¤ ¤ ¤ ¤

Let me talk with you now about what may be one of *your* fears as a parent. You may be apprehensive about recognizing the fears in your children's lives.

Don't be too hard on yourself. Most of us received little or no training in how to be a parent before our children were born. And even if we had, our humanity would still show through. We are not all-knowing and there are no guarantees in parenting. God expects us to do our best, but He doesn't expect us to be perfect.

DEPRESSION

Depression is not a respecter of persons. It can be felt acutely by anyone of any age. It attacks adults, young adults and teenagers; even very young children often show signs of being depressed. Sometimes professional counseling is needed, but many times, simply by following the principles set forth in this chapter, a parent can help either a young child or a teenager through this difficult time.

Depression in Children

Perhaps it seems odd to discuss depression in young children as a problem, but we must be aware that it occurs much more often than we might imagine.

A child's depression often goes undetected by the adults around him. This condition in children is probably hidden more successfully than when it occurs in

any other age group. The child doesn't realize he is depressed, and even if parents suspect that something is wrong, they often deny their child is chronically unhappy. They fail to recognize, accept or respond appropriately to the child's symptoms. After all, who wants to admit his child is depressed?

Recognizing the Symptoms

How can you recognize childhood depression? Here is a composite picture of how a child would appear if every characteristic of depression were included.

First of all, the child would appear quite *unhappy*. He would not verbally complain of this, and he might not even be aware of it, but his behavior would give you that impression.

This sad child also would demonstrate *withdrawal and inhibition*. His interest in normal activities would diminish. He would appear listless, and his parents would think he is bored or sick.

Often concerned parents begin looking for some symptoms of a hidden physical illness, and indeed some *physical symptoms* could further blur the earmarks of depression. These symptoms include headaches, stomach aches and sleeping or eating disturbances.

Discontent is a common mood. The child would give the impression of being dissatisfied. He would derive little pleasure from what he does. People often wonder if someone else is responsible for the way the child feels.

The child would feel *rejected and unloved*. He would tend to withdraw from anything that might be a disappointment to him. As with other age groups, a *negative self-concept* and even feelings of worthlessness would be present.

Irritability and a low frustration tolerance would be seen, but the child would be unaware of why he is upset.

Sometimes, however, he would act just the opposite, attempting to deal with his depressive feelings by *clowning around* and provoking others. He especially may act this way at a time of achievement because he would find it difficult to handle something positive. This provocative behavior makes other people angry.

Now of course, these characteristics will not all be present in every case of a depressed child. When several of them are obvious, though, or any one is particularly intense, depression should be suspected.

Sometimes children will experience and express their depression in the same way as adults, but not always. However, enlightened adults can recognize the symptoms fairly easily. Because of their limited experience and physiology, children tend to express their depression as rebellion, negativity, anger and resentment. The depression expressed when parents divorce, for example, may be manifested by bedwetting, attacking friends or siblings, clinging to parents, failure in school or exaggerated storytelling.

Looking for the Causes

Why do children become depressed? It could be caused by any of the following: a physical defect or illness; malfunction of the endocrine glands; lack of affection, which can create insecurity in the child; lack of positive feedback or encouragement for accomplishments; death of a parent; divorce, separation, or desertion by a parent; parental favor toward a sibling; poor relationship between the child and a step-parent; economic problems in the home; moving to a new home or

school; punishment by others.[1]

Look for any type of loss that may have occurred in the child's life. This could be the loss of a pet or friend, a severe rejection experience, a divorce situation, or a death in the family. A child's thoughts and feelings due to the loss of a parent through divorce probably will be similar to and as intense as those experienced when there is a death. Whatever the type of loss, try to see it from the child's point of view. It is easy to misinterpret a child's perspective, especially if you have not been around children very much.

Differences Due to Child's Age

The signs and symptoms of depression vary with the child's age. Even infants can be depressed, and an infant who is depressed simply may not thrive. Generally, children age two to five are less apt to experience depression than those younger or older. However, a parent's moods may severely affect a small child. For example, a mother who is depressed may withdraw from her child, who in turn also becomes depressed. The problem is that the child usually cannot overcome his depression until the mother overcomes hers.

A Young Child

Depression in a young child is a normal reaction to a perceived loss, and you as the adult need to accept it as such, whatever the cause may be. Allow the child a period of time to adjust to the loss. Let your child know that everyone experiences sadness and depression at one time or another—but be sure to put it into terminology the child can understand. Explain that feelings like this are normal and that in time they will go away and the child will feel better. Encourage him to tell God about his feelings and assure him that God understands

our down times as well as our happy times.

As a child goes through the adjustment process, keep in mind the characteristics of both the magic years of the younger child and the middle years of the older child. A child in either age group will need to:

- accept the pain of the loss;
- remember and review his relationship with the loved person;
- become familiar with all the different feelings that are part of grief: anger, sadness and despair;
- express to others his sorrow, anger and sense of loss;
- verbalize any feelings of guilt;
- find a network of caretakers. He needs many people to support him at this time.[2]

The younger child especially will need to be helped to experience the depression as fully as possible. Resisting or ignoring the depression merely prolongs the experience. Encourage the child to be as honest as possible in expressing his feelings, in admitting that he is depressed or sad, and listen without being judgmental or critical. He needs your support.

If grief is involved, you need to allow the child, no matter what his age, to do the grieving naturally. If the grief is over divorce, do not expect him to get over it quickly. This type can last a long time, and it can recur from time to time.

Help the child find some type of activity that will bolster him. A new game, a sight-seeing trip, or anything that would interest him may be helpful.

Find a way for the child to experience some type of success. Recall what he has done fairly well, and help

him use that special ability again. His self-esteem can be rediscovered and elevated through small successes.

Help the child break out of his routine. Even such simple items as a new food at a meal or taking him to a special restaurant may help. Taking a day off for an outing may be particularly helpful.

A Teenager

John sits staring at the wall. He has been that way for several days. This last week he missed several of his classes, and when he did attend, he sat quietly with very little response. At dinner tonight he picked at his food and left most of it untouched. In fact, he hasn't even eaten with the rest of the family much recently. His friends have stopped calling since he turns down so many of their invitations. What is wrong? John is depressed.

What causes depression in teens? Mostly, the same things that cause depression in adults, with the transitional struggles of adolescence thrown in as well. Let's consider this concern since stress can be connected to depression.

A sense of loss is one of the major themes underlying depression, but it is often overlooked. Being rejected by someone, losing an athletic event, having to wear braces at sixteen, and so on, can be real losses to a teen, though adults may not perceive them as such.

There are other, more serious, losses. When a teen loses a parent in death, for example, he often denies the fact in order to protect himself from the threatening feelings of grief which accompany such a loss. If the relationship was close, there will be intense pain, and even anger at being left alone.

The death of a brother or sister can produce conflicting feelings because of the mixture of positive and negative feelings siblings usually have for one another.

If a teen loses a friend in death, there is intense anxiety. Teenagers are aware that adults die, but the death of a peer is shocking and unnerving. It forces a teen to face his own mortality at an age when he is not prepared to do so.

Another shock that many teens face is the loss of a parent through divorce. When this occurs, the teen loses his security and his confidence in the future. Anger at the parent who left usually is stronger and lasts longer than if the person had died. A teen thinks, *If he had died, he wouldn't have been able to help it. He wouldn't have had a choice. But it's only a divorce, and he had a choice. So why did he leave?*

A teen tends to blame himself to a large degree for his parents' divorce, and the guilt he feels over the part he thinks he played is strong—and difficult to resolve.

Even when a friend moves away, the teen experiences a deep sense of loss. The same sense of loss can occur when the teen himself has to change schools or make some other type of move.[3]

Another factor to consider is that the normal developmental process itself presents teenagers with a number of real losses and threats to their self-esteem. During this time they are expected to loosen their dependence upon their parents. Some are tied closer to Mom and Dad than others and are hesitant to do this, whereas others may break away as fast as they can.

They are also expected to take responsibility for their future and eventually the running of their own

lives. Learning to live without some of the previous sources of gratification can be an underlying factor for depression.

A sudden loss can create in a teen the sense of being out of control and of floundering. A loss that is gradual, even though it may be painful, can be prepared for, at least to some degree.

Often the depression is heightened if what is lost is seen by the teen as necessary and irreplaceable. In his book on counseling the depressed, Archibald Hart, dean of the graduate school of psychology at Fuller Seminary, describes four different types of losses:

Abstract losses are intangible, such as the loss of self-respect, love, hope or ambition. Our minds perceive these losses, and we feel we have experienced them. At times the loss may be real, but it may not be as bad as we feel it is.

Concrete losses involve tangible objects—a home, a car, a parent, a close friend, a photograph or a pet. We could feel and see the object prior to the loss.

Imagined losses are created solely by our active imaginations. We think someone doesn't like us anymore. We think people are talking behind our backs. Teens often excel at this. Their self-talk focuses on negatives and may not be based on fact.

The most difficult type of loss to handle, however, is the *threatened loss.* This loss has not yet occurred, but there is the real possibility that it will happen. To a teen, waiting for the results of a physical exam or waiting to hear from the admissions office of a college to which he has applied carries the possibility of loss. Depression occurs because, in this type of loss, the teen is powerless to do anything about it. In a sense, he

is immobilized.

The Younger Teen

There is a difference between the depression of teens aged thirteen through sixteen or seventeen and that of older adolescents. A young teen will avoid admitting personal concerns and may not exhibit or even experience the hopelessness or self-depreciation adults or older teens feel. A young teen is oriented less to *thinking* about something than *doing* something, and is apt to express or handle depression in one of these three different ways:

1. He will *deny* internal depression, but it can be recognized by excessive fatigue, even after adequate rest; hypochondria (an abnormal concern about normal physical changes going on within him); or an inability to concentrate in school or in other situations.

2. He may be *keeping too busy* in an attempt to keep his mind off of things. He may demonstrate an unnatural need to be with people, or he may prefer to be alone, pursuing his own private activities with tremendous intensity.

3. He may consciously or subconsciously appeal for help through *unacceptable behavior,* which can include tempter tantrums, running away, stealing, or a variety of other rebellious acts. These are usually conducted in such a manner as to ensure his being caught.[4]

The Older Teen

An older teen tends to manifest his depression in ways similar to those of adults. Yet he may still express it indirectly, through maladaptive behavior. How?

Drug use is one means of expression. It helps the

young person defend himself against being depressed. The secrecy of obtaining illegal drugs can add excitement to his life, and sharing the drug experience offers peer relationships.

Sexual promiscuity also is used as a defense against depression, more frequently by girls than boys. They believe that the attention and the feeling of being needed and wanted can overcome their sadness and their loneliness.

Suicidal behavior is another clear manifestation. There has been a significant rise in suicidal behavior and even in actual accomplished suicide among both early and later teens. It may be a reflection of depression, or it could be tied in with other causes, but the family of a depressed teen should be aware of the possibility.

DANGER SIGNALS OF SUICIDE[5]

Suicide is a topic we would all prefer to avoid—but we cannot, especially when we see the increase in the number of adolescent suicides. Every 83 minutes a teenager commits suicide in our country. Those are just the ones we know about.

Each year, the reported cases of attempted suicides for teens is more than 500,000. It is the third major cause of death for adolescents. Sometimes the stress and futility of life (even for Christian youth) seems overwhelming to them and this seems the only answer. When a teen experiences depression, the causes may not be clear to him or to us; thus, there is no clear solution.

Even though most parents are shocked when their teen commits suicide or even makes an attempt to, in retrospect they realize there were warning signs. It is important to take any hint or indication concerning suicide seriously. Here are some danger signals which may help

Guidelines for Helping Depressed Kids

What can you say to your child or teen who is going through depression?

For openers, you can simply say, "I care for you and am available. I want to be with you."

There is healing in the physical touch. An arm around the shoulder, a pat on the back, or taking hold of the hand all convey acceptance. Be honest and tell your child, "I don't understand all that you are going through, but I am trying—and I'm here to help you."

Most people don't know what to do for their depressed kids. Here are some practical guidelines. How closely you follow these will depend upon the intensity and duration of the depression. If it is only for a few hours or a day or two, or if the person is feeling

---

you recognize it if this problem ever arises:

- Often a teen becomes preoccupied with death themes, or expresses suicidal thoughts.
- Sometimes the person will give away prized possessions. He may even make a will or make some other type of final arrangements.
- Severe changes in sleeping habits could be a sign.
- Sudden and extreme changes in eating habits and weight could be a clue.
- Any changes in school attendance or grades, or dropping out of favorite activities, may be a clue.
- Watch for personality changes such as nervousness, outbursts of anger, or apathy regarding health or appearance.
- Use of drugs or alcohol should arouse your suspicions.

down but is still functioning, not all of the suggestions would apply. However, if the depression has lasted for quite a while, and the child is dragging around, not functioning, not eating, or not sleeping, you should apply the appropriate measures.

1. *Understand the causes and symptoms of depression.* If your child is so depressed that he just stares, ignores greetings, or turns away from you, remember that he doesn't want to act that way. In depression, the person loses the ability to govern his thinking and his emotions. If he is severely depressed, he cannot control himself any more than you could walk a straight line after twirling yourself around twenty-five times. Understanding the normal behavior of a depressed person will enable you to control your own responses better and you will be able to help your child more effectively.

- A recent suicide of a friend, relative or admired public figure could be cause for concern if your teen has a weak formation of his own identity. He may identify too much with the deceased and try to follow that person's lead.

- Any previous suicide attempt is serious since the next attempt usually occurs within three months.

- Some teens talk about obtaining guns, knives or other weapons.

- A loss of interest in friends or peers may be significant, especially if it continues.

- Watch out for verbal inuendos such as: "You won't have to worry about me for very long"; or, "I won't bother you anymore"; or, "Maybe it would be better if I were dead"; or, "You'll be sorry. Just wait and see."

    If any of these danger signals continue, be alert. You may need to seek professional help.

2. *Watch out for the possibility of suicide, even with children.* If you even suspect your child may be thinking along this line, take it very seriously. Unfortunately, this tragic problem is on the increase. The family of any depressed person should be aware of the potential of suicide. Realize that any individual who is so depressed that he talks about the utter hopelessness of the future might be considering ending his own life. Every hint or statement or allusion to suicide should be talked about. Ask the child to tell you about his suicidal thoughts or plans. It helps the depressed person if the subject can be brought out into the open. Then he knows that other people are aware and can be called upon for help and support.

3. *Get the depressed child or teen to a doctor if the condition continues.* Your family physician may be able to help, or he may recommend someone who can. The time factor is very important. Don't let depression go on and on. For a teen, you may have to make the arrangements, guide him firmly into the car, and just go!

As long as you tolerate a child or a teen's depression, you help maintain it.

4. *Give the child your full support but don't overreact.* The entire family needs to be made aware of the situation and instructed as to their responses. Confrontation with a depressed teen and strong discipline with a child should be suspended until they achieve greater stability. Ask the family not to attack the person, not to bring up his failures, not to come down hard on him, and not to ask him to do things he is not capable of doing while he is depressed.

5. *Don't avoid the depressed child or teen.* He doesn't have the plague. Avoidance further isolates him and could make him feel worse. You might be avoiding

him because you feel guilty about his depression, thinking you are the cause. Be aware that one person may contribute to another's problem from time to time, but no one person is responsible for another's happiness.

6. *Understand that a depressed child or teen really hurts.* It may be even worse for the younger child since it's hard for him to understand why he feels so bad. Don't suggest to either one that he does not really feel bad or that he is just trying to get your sympathy. Don't tell him to "snap out of it." Don't tell him that all he has to do is "just pray to God about it," or "read the Word more," giving him the impression that any of those actions will solve everything.

Often a depressed person deliberately chooses portions of Scripture that reinforce his feelings of loss and unworthiness. Any Scriptures given to a depressed person must be selected with care.

7. *Empathize, rather than sympathize, with your child or teen.* Sympathy can only reinforce a person's feelings of hopelessness. It may make him feel even more helpless and may lower his already low self-esteem. Statements such as, "It's so awful that you are depressed"; or, "You must feel miserable"; or, "How could this ever happen?" rarely help.

8. *Make sure he eats.* If he doesn't want to eat, you can say, "Look, you may not feel like eating, but you probably are hungry. Starving won't help. Food is important, so let's eat now. I'll sit down and eat with you, and then let's talk about what's troubling you."

Don't harp on the food problem, though, or on his eating habits. Saying, "You'll make me feel bad if you don't eat this food"; or, "Think of all the starving people in China," won't get him to eat. Instead, it will probably make him feel worse. Remember, not eating

is a symptom of being depressed.

9. *Keep the person busy.* This is one of the best things you can do for him. Physical activity during severe depression can be more beneficial than mental activity.

The activities planned should be those that he has enjoyed in the past, with all preparations made in detail. If he has lost interest in those activities, gently remind him of the fun he had before with them and then firmly and positively insist that he become involved. Don't ask him if he would like to, because he might not know, or he may not care to respond. Don't get angry and say, "You're going with me because I'm sick and tired of you sitting around feeling sorry for yourself." Rather, you could say, "I know you haven't been feeling well, but you are entitled to some enjoyment. I think you might like this once we get started. And I would like to share this activity with you."

Perhaps you could call to find out what time a school game or activity begins. Upon hanging up you say to your teen or child, "I think we can get ready for it, so let's start now." If you are going shopping, you could suggest, "Come along. I like to have someone with me, and I need your advice."

Any activity can be used, but be aware that you may need to schedule his entire day for him. By getting him involved, you can help him begin to break destructive behavior patterns, and this helps him gain energy and motivation.

10. *Don't ever tease your child or teen, or lecture him, about his lack of confidence.* However, don't ignore it either. Loss of self-esteem is common in depression, and it must be faced. In reactivating confidence, help the child see the lack of logic of his self-disparagement,

but don't do it by berating or arguing. Also, don't join in his self-pity. Rather, look for past accomplishments and get him to focus on what he was able to do. You can say, "Perhaps you can't do some things the way you did before, but let's talk about the things you still do well. What do you think they are?"

If he says, "I can't do anything," gently name something he can do, or try to draw it out of him. At this point you are trying to help him overcome his sense of helplessness.

Be persistent and steady in your responses to the child's depression. Remember that, at this point, you have more control over your emotional responses than he has over his.

If the depression is severe and the child does not respond, he should have professional help. However, a parent can help a child handle many depressive experiences without taking him for counseling. By following these principles, you will be much more able to fulfill the biblical teaching on giving empathy and encouragement, and you will be guiding your child toward a considerably more positive attitude toward life.

> Bear one another's burdens, and thus fulfill the law of Christ (Galatians 6:2).

> Therefore encourage one another, and build up one another, just as you also are doing (1 Thessalonians 5:11).

¤¤¤ 7 ¤¤¤

DIVORCE

One of the most stressful things that happens to children is the divorce of their parents. That can be the most traumatic experience a child will ever have to face.

Newsweek magazine has estimated that 45 percent of all children will live with only one parent at some time before they are eighteen. Twelve million children now under the age of eighteen have parents who are divorced.

The effects of divorce on children have been shown to be more serious and longer lasting than many divorced parents are willing to admit. Studies released in England in 1978 showed that children of divorce have a shorter life expectancy and more illness than those in families where no divorce occurred. These children leave school earlier as well In New York City, which has a very high adolescent suicide rate, two of every

three teenage suicides involve teenagers whose parents are divorced. Many other teens carry a pattern of insecurity, depression anxiety, and anger into their adult years.[1] On the average it takes a child up to five years to adjust to the impact of his parents' divorce.[2]

What a Child Loses

In a divorce, children experience many losses. These can include not only the loss of one of the parents, but also the loss of home, neighborhood, school friends, family standard of living, family outings, family holiday get-togethers, and so on.

A child's self-esteem is in serious jeopardy, too. Have you ever wondered what it would be like to learn, as a child, that your parents are divorcing, feel the panic of it, and then have to face telling your friends? Fear becomes a daily companion, and the losses multiply.

When a child loses a parent, he also may lose his hope for the future. Because of the uncertainty, a child can feel out of control to a greater extent than ever before. The parents upon whom he depended are no longer the solid rock he needs, and the shakiness of his situation can soon show up in such areas as family finances. If a divorced father has promised to take care of the family and his monthly payments become irregular, and then eventually cease, the child's uncertainty becomes more acute—and what emotional loss must he feel regarding his father's apparent lack of concern for him? This is an additional stressor.

How Age Affects Reactions

Divorce affects children in different ways depending upon the age of the child.

Young children of *three to five,* and even younger,

become fearful; the routine separations of life become traumatic. A parent's going shopping or the child's leaving for preschool is a stressful experience.

These children tend to regress to earlier behavior patterns and become more passive and dependent. More and more they ask questions like, "What's that?" in an effort to overcome the disorganization of the crisis. They have a great need for affection. They may refuse to feed themselves, and some even revert to a need for diapers. They can create wild and imaginative fantasies in their minds because they are puzzled by what is happening to them. They are bewildered. Play does not have the same sense of fun. These preschoolers may become aggressive with other children.

In addition, some psychologists believe that the absence of a parent of the opposite sex could be damaging to the child's sexual development. A child learns about sexuality and male/female responses by observing the interaction between his mother and father. A positive role model helps create the image of how he or she is to respond in the future.

For example, the first man in a girl's life is her father. Through his interactions, she learns how to respond to men in her life. A healthy, positive relationship helps her obtain the balance she needs. If Father is either absent or a "phantom father" (he is there but uninvolved), she may develop a fear response toward men or become over-involved with every man she encounters. (For more information on this topic, see *Always Daddy's Girl* by this author.[3])

On the other side, I have talked with men who were raised without a mother or sisters and as a result were at a loss in being able to develop healthy relationships with women in their own lives.

When you are counseling a three- to five-year-old child whose parents are divorcing, help the child verbalize his hurt and his idea of why his parents are divorcing. Throughout all the stages of childhood, a common thought is, *Did I cause my parent's divorce? Am I responsible for not having a family any more?* As we mentioned before, a child this young has unrealistic perceptions and may feel as though his behavior or thoughts actually caused the divorce. It is not easy to convince him otherwise, but it is vital to try to help him see other possibilities.

The *six- to eight-year-old* has his own set of reactions. Sadness is there, and his sense of responsibility for the parents' breakup is stronger. His feelings of loss are deep. He is afraid of being abandoned, and sometimes even of starving. He yearns for the parent who has left.

Frequently these children are angry with the parent who cares for them all the time. They have conflicting loyalties. They want to love both parents, but they struggle with the feeling that loving one is being disloyal to the other. Thus they feel torn and confused. Symptoms can include nail biting, bedwetting, loss of sleep, and retreating into fantasy to solve family problems. Children of both age groups become possessive.

Preadolescent children of *nine to twelve* usually experience anger as their main emotional reaction. This anger is felt toward the one the child feels is responsible for the family breakup, who could be the custodial parent. However, instead of leveling his anger directly at the parent, he may aim it at his peers, alienating them at the time he needs them most.

The child of this age also suffers from a badly

shaken self-image. Some of these children will throw themselves into what they are doing with great intensity as their way of combatting that and of handling the disruption of their lives.

Teens, when a divorce occurs, respond largely on the basis of their own personalities and weaknesses which have already developed. If their home is no longer a safe retreat, they may tend to spend more and more time away. They may feel pressured to mature too rapidly and take on adult responsibilities or behaviors before they are ready. Because of this, some may rebel with childish behavior. If parental supervision is inadequate, they can get into real trouble.

When their parents begin to date again, teens may feel threatened since this brings into focus the fact that their parents are sexual beings and have their own set of needs. If a parent is upset, a teen may want to help but not know how. Or a parent could dump his or her frustration and upset upon the teen who is not capable of dealing with these adult issues.

The normal concerns of teens intensify because their world is shattered–and what happens to the values they have been taught? Most parents teach their children that marriage is for life—and now they are divorced. You can see why a teen would be confused and disillusioned.

A Child's Two Main Concerns

In the turmoil of divorce, children of all ages have two major concerns.

The **first** is their *dream that their parents will reconcile*. The children believe that if this were to happen, all their problems would be over. They think that,

in spite of previous problems, the family was better off when both parents were there. The child may have seen the conflict, but he is willing to tolerate it in order to have an intact family. After all, this is the only family he knows.

His **second** concern revolves around himself— *what will happen to him?* He is afraid that the parent he is living with will abandon him. One parent already did. Why shouldn't the other?

If one parent was forced to leave (as many are), the child's fear centers on being thrown out as his mother or father was. Again this is a stressor.

Another fear concerns being replaced in the parents' affection by someone else. As the custodial parent begins to date, the child wonders if this new person is going to become important to his parent. If so, will he lose the time and attention he now receives?

Emotional Stages of Reaction

In order to help the child of a divorced couple, it is important to understand what he experiences. Remember that his feelings will change with the passage of time. There are fairly clear emotional stages through which a child passes as he struggles to understand and deal with a divorce. These stages are normal, and they cannot be avoided or bypassed. They have nothing to do with the spirituality of the child. Your goal, in endeavoring to help the child, is to guide him as he passes through these stages in order to minimize the negative effects and produce positive growth.

Shock. Although a child's home may be filled with visible conflict, the child rarely expects his parents to get a divorce. He may not like the conflict, but he hopes it will settle down eventually. Discovering that a

separation or divorce is going to happen is usually a great shock to a child.

Fear and anxiety. These unsettling emotions will occur because the child is now faced with an unknown future. In the past a home and family with two parents have been the child's source of stability. Those are now about to be shattered.

Fear and anxiety may manifest themselves in restlessness, nightmares, sleeplessness, stomach problems, sweating, and aches and pains. These are normal problems. A child needs to be given reassurance. It is important to give him the facts, because a child's imagination may run wild, and knowing is better than wondering. A child may tend to think up worse problems than actually exist.

Feeling abandoned and rejected. After fear and anxiety come feelings of abandonment and rejection. The feelings of the initial stage recede and are replaced by this struggle. The child may know at one level that he will not be rejected or abandoned, but at a deeper level he is still concerned that it might happen. A younger child has difficulty distinguishing between the parents leaving one another and their leaving him, and he may focus on this. This stage of the child's emotions may be perpetuated by unkept promises on the part of the parent who leaves.

Loneliness and sadness. Feeling sad and alone soon replaces the sense of abandonment and rejection. As the family structure changes and calms down, the reality of what has occurred begins to settle in. A child sometimes feels this stage with a pain in the stomach and a tightness in the chest. This is when depression begins and regular activities tend to be neglected. Many children do a lot of thinking, which is usually wishful

daydreaming. These fantasies follow the same theme—
parents get together again and everything is all right.
Crying spells may become more frequent at this time.

Frustration and anger. These feelings are the
next to come—children whose parents divorce or separate become angry children. This is a natural response
to the frustrations they feel. In addition, they have seen
upset and angry parents, and the children emulate this
modeling of anger. The anger may continue to be the
pattern for many years and, unless dealt with and
resolved, probably will carry over into adult relationships.

The child's anger is there for several reasons. It
serves as a protection and a warning signal, just like
depression. It is often a reaction to hurt, fear or frustration, and it alerts others to the fact that there is a
problem.

The anger may not show itself directly. It's an
inner, basic feeling which, rather than being expressed
openly, may be suppressed or masked. It may become
evident, then, through a negative perspective on life, or
through irritability, or withdrawal and self-isolation.
Anger also may be expressed through strong resistance—to school, or chores, or whatever the child wants
to resist.

Anger is an involuntary response, so don't be
threatened by it or attempt to deny its presence in the
child. Rather, help the child learn to express and drain
it. According to his ability, help him to understand the
cause for his anger, and its purpose. If it is not allowed
a direct expression, it can come out in an indirect manner, and may erupt in violence. This exhibition would
indicate displaced anger and is far more dangerous than
allowing a child to acknowledge his anger and speak

openly about it.

Resentment and rejection (by the child). Eventually the child's anger moves to resentment and results in his doing the rejecting. He is not over his angry feelings but is now attempting to create some emotional distance between himself and his parent. This is a protective device. Pouting can be one of his forms of rejection, as can the silent treatment. The child won't respond to suggestions or commands, and he often "forgets" to follow through with what he is supposed to do. He becomes hypercritical as well.

This behavior is actually a reaction formation. As a child pushes a parent away, he really wants to be close to the parent. He makes hateful statements and yet wants to be loving. He is trying to protect himself from being rejected, so he rejects first.

Reestablishing trust. The final stage for a child in the problem of dealing with parental divorce is the reestablishment of trust. It is difficult to say how long this will take, as it varies with each situation and child, and can range from months to years.

Helping Your Kids Through These Stages

What can parents or adults do to help? Here are some suggestions:

1. Do not be so concerned with your own feelings that you neglect the child's feelings. Give him some time each day to discuss what he is experiencing and feeling.

2. Allow the child time to process his feelings. There are no quick solutions or cures.

3. A stable environment is beneficial to the child no matter what his age. It's better for him not to have

to move but to live with his remaining parent in the same home and neighborhood with as many things as possible staying the same. Of course, some change will be necessary, and the child will need to adapt, but the parent must realize that the greater the change, the greater the stress and discomfort to the child or teen.

4. Give positive feedback to the child, and build his sense of self-confidence.

5. Reassure him that he is not the cause of the divorce or separation. Both parents need to give him consistent and equal amounts of love.

6. According to the child's level of understanding, help him to know in advance the different types of feelings he will be experiencing. Keep the child informed at all times of any environmental changes expected so he can be prepared.

A child needs to be assured that even though his mother and father will be working through their own struggles as the divorce proceeds, they still will be taking care of him. Parents, friends, and other relatives need to repeat this to the child often so he begins to realize that more than one person is supporting him with this belief. This is an especially appropriate time to assist the child to select some interesting task he can accomplish that will help him overcome his feelings of helplessness and of being out of control.[4]

Blended Families

Some people see remarriage as an answer to their difficulties. Unfortunately, blended families have their own style of stresses and problems. It appears that infants and young children make blended family adjustments a bit easier than teens. It's important to realize

that even though you may see your teenager "changing," a teen thrives on stability and sameness. For example, could you listen to the same record day in and day out for twenty weeks? He does.

In most divorces a teen sees what happened as a personal rejection. Because of this he or she has learned to close up—and then, when the parent remarries, he is expected to open up!

A teen involved in the remarriage of a parent has a number of questions. Some of them are:

"How often will I see my real parent now?"

"Will my real parent feel that I have 'sold out' if I show positive feelings toward my new stepparent?"

"Why do I have to share my real mom or dad with these other kids who have invaded my home?"

"Why can't I have as much time with my own parent as I did when there was no stepparent around?"

Many come to the conclusion that life is not fair, and they can't wait to get old enough to leave home. A blended family often brings more new losses for a teen than it does gains.

One stress experienced particularly by teens is brought about by grieving over the parent who leaves and then facing the problem of divided loyalties. Teens value loyalty, so to love or care about a stepparent could seem disloyal to the teen. Teens need time to express their feelings and should be encouraged to do so. A blended family works best when expectations, fears, concerns and even resentments are anticipated and dealt with prior to the remarriage.

¤¤¤ 8 ¤¤¤

HELPING CHILDREN HANDLE THEIR STRESS

For adults, teens, and children alike, stressors are a part of daily life and we don't worry about most of them. When a child breaks a finger, we have it set and assume it will heal. With chicken pox, we wait for him to get well. When he has a cold, we know he will recover.

When a child has an ulcer, however, or excessive fatigue, or a psychosomatic illness, that's a different matter. It's not so easy to deal with these conditions — which are caused by stress.

Four Ways of Coping

How do children approach life's stressors? They basically follow the same pattern we adults follow. There are four main ways in which we all try to cope:

1. We attempt to remove the stressor.
2. We decide to refuse to allow neutral situations to become stressors.
3. We try to deal directly with the stressor.
4. We look for ways of relaxing to ease the tension of the stress.

Both adults and children use these methods every day. Let's look a little more closely at each method as it relates to a child.

1. We attempt to remove the stressor.

Can a child *remove a stressor?* Occasionally, but usually he doesn't have the necessary power or control. In fact, children often are stuck—with no hope of removal—in a situation which becomes a source of intense stress, so they deal with it by inventing means of getting out of its way. A child may give up his friends because their behavior either is contrary to his standards or it is frightening to him—or both. Or, during a family fight he may go to his room and turn up his radio to drown out the noise.

2. We decide to refuse to allow neutral situations to become stressors.

As for *neutral situations* in a child's life, they sometimes get turned into stressors by other people. Exams at school are a case in point. They can be the source of acceptance or rejection by significant adults such as the child's teachers or parents. Some children worry about the exam, whereas other children refuse to let it pressure them by making statements to themselves like, "Why shouldn't I get a fairly good grade? I've studied and I've done all right so far. And even if I don't, it isn't the end of the world. I'm still okay."

3. *We try to deal directly with the stressor.*

What about *confronting a stressor* head-on and dealing directly with it? That may take figuring out a way to get around it. A child who is tired of being kidded about being heavy can go on a diet and lose weight. I saw a child in a class go to a teacher and ask to have his seat moved because he talked too much to his friend who sat next to him, and he was tired of getting into trouble for it.

4. *We look for ways of relaxing to ease the tension of the stress.*

What about *relaxation?* How can children find a way to ease the tension when stress is facing them? How do *you* relax? Do you jog, play tennis, run, read a novel? These hobbies and activities which give us enjoyment are a source of relaxation for us.

Have you taken your child to the public library and introduced him to the wealth of material found on the shelves? Learning to read novels at an early age may provide one source of relaxation for him. You can help him find others.

Unfortunately, we often structure our children's activities so strictly that they have little time just to be kids. After-school sports are often overly competitive with an emphasis upon winning instead of on the enjoyment of the activity. We adults tend to be result-oriented rather than to do things just for the joy of it, and we project that philosophy onto our children. Yet the child needs a model in relaxation from us. Tim Hansel's book *When I Relax I Feel Guilty*[1] will assist you in helping your child find some good ways to relax.

Many children feel just what this little poem reflects:

I wish I was a rock, a-settin' on a hill;
I wasn't doin' nothin' but just a-settin' still.
I wouldn't eat; I wouldn't sleep;
I wouldn't even wash.
Just set there for a thousand years or so
And rest myself, by gosh!

(Source unknown)

To consider further those four ways of handling stress, answer each of the four questions in the first list below. Then ask your child to answer the next list of questions.

1. How do you see your child removing stressors in his or her life?
2. How do you see your child refusing to allow neutral situations to become stressors?
3. How do you see your child dealing directly with stressors?
4. How do you see your child relaxing?

Now ask your child:

1. How do you handle upsets and frustrations?
2. How do you refuse to let some problems upset you?
3. How do you handle a problem head-on?
4. What's the best way for you to relax?

(You may have to change the wording of some of these, depending upon the age of your child.)

Helping Children Learn

How can we help our children learn to handle the stressors of today more successfully?

One of the best descriptions I have heard of help-

ing a young child is that it is like working on a jigsaw puzzle. You ask him to find the pieces; you point some of them out, and you help him fit the pieces together.

Here are some practical things you can observe as you attempt to help your child cope with the disappointments and stresses in his life.

As an adult, you need to *use the child's language* and be flexible in your communication. You must actively guide your conversation with a young child or you will end up failing to communicate. In working with your child, you need to make your statements very clear and even rephrase them several times. Repeat and repeat patiently. What may be clear to you simply may not register with your child.

Young children have one-track minds, often focusing on one aspect of an event to the exclusion of all others. They cannot see the forest for the trees. If you throw too much information and too many events at a child in one conversation, he cannot handle it. You need to *introduce other aspects of the situation gradually* as he is ready to take them on. Your task is to help the child see all the aspects, organize his thoughts, and explore other possible reasons for the stressful situation.

Whenever you try to help a young child, *remember these facts:* The child feels responsible for what has happened to initiate the stress; he makes connections different from the ones you make; he is egocentric; he has unrealistic and immature perceptions.

If this is how children think, what can you as a parent or teacher do to help this child who is under stress? Sometimes it will be impossible to fully change the child's pattern of thinking. You need to accept this as a fact of life and lessen your own frustration. *Helping a child fully express his inner thoughts and feelings*

is one of the best approaches. It helps him gain greater self-control in a crisis event. By expressing his thoughts aloud, he can move to a new position. Patiently repeat your questions to the child, and encourage him to think aloud. Help him uncover the real or most probable reason for what is occurring. Try to help him discover this himself instead of giving him the reason. Look for any indications of guilt he may be experiencing.

A child needs time alone with his parent each week. This can be difficult if there are several children in the family, but it is needed. Parents need to be good listeners and help their child express his feelings, which in turn will help resolve his anger and frustrations. One of the best ways a child learns to handle stress is through observation within the home whether the family consists of both parents, one parent and a dog, grandparents, or those in a foster home. The positive attitude and modeling of the important adults in a child's life will give the child a firm foundation for dealing with the stresses of his life. (Since I am assuming that you are an adult reading this book, let me suggest two additional resources for your own reading: *Less Stress* by Dave and Jan Congo;[2] and my book, *How to Have a Creative Crisis*.[3] In this latter book, see the chapter on the questions of life.)

Children Who Cope

Children who are able to cope with the stressors of life accept their strengths and their limitations. They are also individualistic. They respond to peers, and they have a number of friends, but they still maintain their own individual identity.

In contrast, peer-oriented children are less sure of themselves and have a lower opinion of themselves.

Because peer pressure becomes so influential during adolescent years, preadolescent children must become aware of and able to maintain their own identity.

Children who cope are able to express their feelings. They can share their hopes, anger, hurts, frustrations and joys. They don't bottle up their feelings.[4]

If your child struggles with this, sit down with him, listen to his feelings of disappointment, and work with him on the alternatives. You may want to come up with a few suggestions including the ridiculous as well as the serious.

One eight-year-old boy wanted to do something, and he was disappointed and upset because he couldn't. His mother said, "I know five different ways you can handle this disappointment, Billy, and some of them may work. If you want to hear them, let me know."

In ten minutes he was back, asking.

"You really want to know?" his mother asked.

Billy grumbled and said, "Yes."

"Well," she said, "here they are. Maybe some are all right and maybe some aren't." She sat down with him and shared the following:

1. "I could go to my room and throw my clothes out the window to show everyone I'm upset."
2. "I could write a letter to God telling Him how disappointed I am and then read it to a friend."
3. "I could call eleven of my friends and complain to each of them."
4. "I could set the timer on the clock and cry for forty minutes until the bell rings."
5. "I could tell my mom that I'm disappointed and then we could talk about what we could do in-

stead and maybe plan for this activity another time."

This mother and son ended up with a very interesting discussion.

Like some adults, some children are not overly affected by the stressors of life. Why? Which children seem to handle the stressors of life best? They all seem to have some of the same characteristics.

- They can concentrate instead of jumping around from one thing to another.

- They can handle frustration.

- They can work at a job until it is finished.

- They have learned to accept the disappointments of life, or they find alternatives.

- They are able to postpone gratification. This is an important key. The children who handle stress well are those who can wait.

The Word of God

In addition to what we have discussed before, helping a child understand, commit to memory, and apply significant passages from the Word of God to his life is probably the most effective solution to stress.

A few of the passages which can become a source of stability and comfort to a child are:

James 1:2,3—Consider it all joy, my brethren, when you encounter various trials, knowing that the testing of your faith produces endurance.

Philippians 4:6-9—Be anxious for nothing, but in everything by prayer and supplication with thanksgiving let your requests be made known to God.

And the peace of God, which surpasses all comprehension, shall guard your hearts and your minds in Christ Jesus.

Finally, brethren, whatever is true, whatever is honorable, whatever is right, whatever is pure, whatever is lovely, whatever is of good repute, if there is any excellence and if anything worthy of praise, let your mind dwell on these things. The things you have learned and received and heard and seen in me, practice these things; and the God of peace shall be with you.

Psalm 37:1-9 — Do not fret because of evildoers.
Be not envious toward wrongdoers.
For they will wither quickly like the grass,
And fade like the green herb.
Trust in the LORD, and do good;
Dwell in the land and cultivate faithfulness.
Delight yourself in the LORD;
And He will give you the desires of your heart,
Commit your way to the LORD.
Trust also in Him, and He will do it.
And He will bring forth your righteousness as
    the light,
And your judgment as the noonday.
Rest in the LORD and wait patiently for Him;
Do not fret because of him who prospers in his way,
Because of the man who carries out wicked
    schemes.
Cease from anger, and forsake wrath;
Do not fret, it leads only to evildoing.
For evildoers will be cut off,
But those who wait for the LORD, they will inherit
    the land.

1 Peter 5:7—Casting all your anxiety upon Him, because He cares for you.

Isaiah 41:10,13—Do not fear, for I am with you;
Do not anxiously look about you, for I am your God.
I will strengthen you, surely I will help you.
Surely I will uphold you with My righteous right hand. . . .
For I am the LORD your God, who upholds your right hand,
Who says to you, "Do not fear, I will help you."

Psalm 27:1—The LORD is my light and my salvation; Whom shall I fear?
The LORD is the defense of my life;
Whom shall I dread?

Isaiah 26:3—The steadfast of mind Thou wilt keep in perfect peace, Because he trusts in Thee.

Psalm 4:8—In peace I will both lie down and sleep,
For Thou alone, O LORD, dost make me to dwell in safety.

Hebrews 13:6—The Lord is my helper, I will not be afraid. What shall man do to me?

Read these verses again. Write out how you would explain the meaning of each verse to a child. How would you help that child apply the passage to his own situation?

The child will learn best by seeing the reality of these passages lived out in the life of another individual. He needs to see the powerful effect of Scripture, and he needs to see that it does make a difference when a person puts into practice what God's Word has to say.

¤¤¤ 9 ¤¤¤

HELPING TEENS HANDLE THEIR STRESS

For teens, frustrations come in many packages, large and small. They're frustrated (and then stressed) by being thwarted, blocked, disappointed, etc. If they're hungry and can't eat, they get frustrated. If they want to join an elite club at school and are unable to do so, they become frustrated. If they try to untangle the mixed messages they receive about sex, they become frustrated.

Stress and Self-Talk

But do you really know why they get frustrated? It's because they have not learned to handle life when it doesn't go their way. Often they say, "Boy, do I want that," when in reality they are thinking, *I must have that. I've got to have it or my whole world will crumble. If I don't get it, the result will be total disaster. I've got*

to have my way! This can include anything—a grade on an exam, making the team, having a pimple clear up before a date, having hair turn out right, etc. The list is endless. Many teens have not learned to say, "Boy, I really want that—but if I don't get it, it's not the end of the world. I may be disappointed and feel down for a while, but it's not going to cripple me. I can adjust and live without it and move ahead."

Much of the time our frustrations and stresses occur because of what we say to ourselves. This is called self-talk. All of us, children, teens and adults alike, talk to ourselves. When a teen learns to change his self-talk and his ways of responding when frustrated, he will experience less stress.

A person's perceptions and evaluations of the world around him as they relate to his own self-confidence actually can cause stress. Changing self-talk may be difficult but it also may be the best way to reduce stress, tension and anxiety.

Giving It Permission

One of the most important strategies for handling frustration and stress with self-talk is to give the situation permission to happen. When you resist something that is inevitable, it just persists and you become upset. Listen to this interaction between one parent and his teen:

JOHN: I was so upset today, I couldn't even think straight during my last two classes. I am really bummed out.

DAD: What happened? Do you want to tell me about it?

JOHN: I took most of my lunch hour to wait in line for those tickets we need, and after a half hour,

they closed the window and said there were no more. And since I waited I was late for my next class.

John went on sharing his frustration and after a while his dad said, "How do you feel about your reaction to what happened? I can understand how that can be frustrating, but what do you think now?"

JOHN: I wish it hadn't happened and I wish I hadn't gotten so upset.

DAD: Want a wild suggestion?

JOHN: Well, it couldn't be any worse than what I went through.

DAD: There was nothing you could do to control what happened or to stop it, was there?

JOHN: No, not really.

DAD: And you probably felt you were being dumped on and it was unfair?

JOHN: Yeah. You bet.

DAD: Well, since there was nothing you could do, I wonder what might happen if you give it permission to have happened and just go with it?

JOHN: What?! How would that help? That is worse than what I did!

DAD: Well, you could say to yourself, "This isn't what I wanted to happen, but it has. And I don't want it to upset me so much, so I'll go with it. I'll just say it's unfortunate, but I can accept it. I can handle the disappointment. In fact, I'll even give it permission to happen." If you said that, you'd be more in control of what was happening and how you were feeling. It's just a thought. You may want to use it sometime.

This works! I have seen it work in countless situations — with adults and with teens. We can't apply it to everything that happens, but we can to a lot of things. Have you ever given yourself permission to be stuck in traffic, to be late for an appointment, or to flub the lines when you're talking? Try it. The inner response certainly will be less stressful than fighting the problem.

Ways to Help

There are three approaches you could use to help your teen handle his stress. Two of the ways offer only temporary help or no help at all. The third is the best.

First, you could encourage him to change his environment in order to prevent things that are likely to produce stress. This might include changing part-time jobs, changing friends, church, school, time spent with step-parents, etc. Unfortunately, most people do not realize how many additional changes would be involved with each of the above, and those could create even more stress. Not a very good method.

The second approach would be to teach your teen to recognize and do something about the symptoms. Any of us can attempt to alter our emotional and physiological responses to stress by using medication, tranquilizers, relaxation techniques, meditation or imagery. Not a very good method either.

Here is the third approach to helping a teen handle stress, and I'm sure you will agree it is the best way. It is: Help him learn to alter his assumptions and negative ways of thinking. These are what make him more vulnerable to stress.

Along with showing them alternate ways of interpreting life's frustrations, what other things can

parents do to help their teens handle stress? Many times we can't change their environment or the other pressures of their lives outside the home, but we can assist them in their efforts to develop coping skills. And within the family we can make the changes necessary to ensure a positive environment.

Establishing Rules

One of the best ways to assist a teen is to help him distinguish between what he wants and what he needs. It is often helpful to a teen for an adult to say no. Parents have that right. It may mean a confrontation or bucking peer pressure, but those actions are sometimes necessary.

Remember, any rule you make must be enforceable. Here are two guidelines to follow in establishing rules with a teen:

1. *Share with him the principle behind the rule.*

Saying he doesn't need to know the reason does little to help him think—to consider the pros and cons of what he wants to do versus what you want him to do.

2. *Enlist your teen's help in establishing the rule when it is appropriate.*

We did this years ago just prior to our daughter's learning to drive. Here is what all three of us came up with at a family council meeting:

DRIVING AGREEMENT

1. Before using either car, I will ask my mom or dad if I can use it and explain the purpose.
2. If I want to go somewhere for myself, my homework and piano practicing must be completed first.
3. During the first six months of driving with my own license, I will not use the radio while driving.

4. During the school year, I will be allowed to drive to church on Wednesday nights but cannot take anyone home without prior permission.

5. I will not allow anyone else to use the car under any circumstances.

6. I will be allowed up to thirty-five miles a week and after that I must pay for any additional mileage.

7. I will not carry more than five passengers at any time in the Plymouth nor more than three in the Audi.

8. Upon receiving my driver's permit I will be allowed to drive to church and run local errands when either Mom or Dad is along. I will assist in driving for extended periods of time or on long vacations under all types of driving conditions.

9. I will not give rides to hitchhikers under any conditions nor will I accept a ride if I should have any difficulty with the car.

10. I will either wash the car myself or have it done once every three weeks.

11. I will pay half the increase of the insurance costs and in case of an accident I will assume half the deductible cost.

Handling Type A Stress

Think back with me to the three kinds of stress described earlier—Types A, B and C. Remember that Type A is foreseeable and avoidable. Even though teens may be aware of what's coming, they still tend to worry about how to actually handle the situation. Hear some of their concerns:

"How do I prepare for that crazy midterm exam?"

"How do I turn down that dull job my uncle is offering me?"

"I just know Jeff is going to ask me to

the prom. He's nice as a friend, but I'm
hoping Jim will ask me. How do I turn Jeff
down without hurting him?"

If you were the teen's parent, what would you
say? Would you make suggestions? Tell him or her what
to do? Or draw out of your teen his own ideas?

Why not suggest a plan he could implement
when you're not around? Here is a simple approach in-
volving only three steps:

1. Identify the stress. For a teen, this is probably
   the easiest of these three steps.
2. Explore your options. This is usually the most
   difficult.
3. Take the necessary action. Sometimes easy,
   sometimes not.

For example, you might encourage your teen to
brainstorm aloud his options for handling the job offer
from his uncle. He could:

—Just not respond and avoid (bad choice).
—Ask Mom or Dad to turn it down for him
  (another bad choice).
—Take the job out of obligation and tough
  it out (still a bad choice since it does not
  teach him how to confront a problem
  honestly—nor do the preceding two).
—Say to the uncle, "Thank you for the
  offer. I've considered it but have decided
  I won't be taking the job. It doesn't really
  fit the direction I'm going. I'm disappointed that I won't be with you as much
  as I wanted."

The Broken-Record Technique

As for the date invitation, the less said the better when turning it down. The more reasons a teen gives, the more control she gives the person asking and the more she weakens her own position. A response to a date invitation could be, "I'm sorry, but I'm unable to go with you that evening." If the person asks why not, the teen can answer with the same response: "I'm sorry, but I am unable to go with you that night."

If invited to use alcohol or drugs, a simple response is sufficient, such as, "No, thanks. I don't use that—and I don't want to try it."

No matter what kind of statements or pressure tactics others use, if the teen simply repeats his statement over and over, he will stay in control. This is called the broken-record technique. It involves *not* telling "why." We have the freedom not to give our reasons. By doing this, a teen will have more resistance to the peer group.

Encourage your teen to work out the problem by himself. If you take over a teen's responsibilities, you delay his experiences of becoming an adult. Help him stand on his own and make his own decisions.

Handling Types B and C Stress

Learning to handle the difficulties of Type B stress, the unforeseeable and unavoidable, will be a lifelong process. The best way to help your teen is:

1. Understand the normal phases a person goes through in a crisis.
2. Develop a biblical perspective on life's crises yourself.
3. Begin to share this information with your teen

as early in his life as possible. How? Read *How to Have a Creative Crisis* by this author.[1] You and your teen could read that book—along with this one—together.

I like what Chuck Swindoll says about crisis:

> Crisis crushes. And in crushing, it often refines and purifies. You may be discouraged today because the crushing has not yet led to a surrender. However, I've stood beside too many of the dying, ministered to too many of the broken and bruised to believe that crushing is an end in itself. Unfortunately, it usually takes the brutal blows of affliction to soften and penetrate hard hearts, though such blows often seem unfair.... After crises crush sufficiently, God steps in to comfort and teach.[2]

Many of the Type C stresses, the foreseeable but unavoidable, occur because of what a person has to do. This is where developing good problem-solving skills will make a difference.[3]

How can you assist your teen in handling Type C stress? First of all, what does he see in you? Do we as parents reflect a positive model in handling our own daily frustrations?

Four-Step Problem Solving

Let me suggest a very simple method of problem-solving you can share with your teen. Some basic questions are involved in this four-step process:

FOUR-STEP PROBLEM SOLVING PROCESS

Step 1—What is my problem?

Your teen is faced with the problem of studying for an important midterm exam, the results of which

are vital for college entrance. Then he receives an invitation to go, at the same time, with a friend who won an all-expense-paid weekend ski trip for two.

Step 2—How can this be solved?
What are my alternatives?

Choice one and the consequences: The teen can go on the ski trip, which probably would never occur again because of the unique circumstances. The consequences are quite obvious—not being prepared for the exam and perhaps not having the grades for college.

Choice two: Stay home and study for the exam and perhaps have a chance for college (that is, if he can keep his mind on studying and not mope about missing the trip).

Choice three: Study as much as possible before and on the trip. This would necessitate letting the friend know how important the studying is. It could also involve studying in the car and perhaps isolating himself at times in order to study. Question: Has the teen ever done this before, and is it worth the risk? Does he have the self-discipline to do it?

Step 3—What is my plan for solving this?

The teen will need to make a choice and then come up with a detailed plan (in writing) in order to follow through. Believe it or not, there are some teens who could carry out this choice.

Step 4—What will the results be?

It is important to both *anticipate* the results of a choice and then *evaluate* the actual results afterward. To help the teen project possible results, ask him questions like, "If you did that, what do you think would be the result?" Or, "What have you tried before, and

what's something new that you haven't thought of yet that would bring different results?" Or, "What else might you try?" And, "What could you do then?"[4]

Helping your teen become aware of his options will help him handle and lessen the stresses in his life.

Building Your Teen's Self-Esteem

Your teen was not born with his (or her) self-concept but it has been in the process of formation for years. As others approved or disapproved of him, he developed an inner opinion of himself. For example, if a child grows up with a critical parent, he may incorporate that parent's attitude within himself and then respond to himself in that same critical way for the rest of his life.

It may not help now to say that the emphasis on self-esteem and identity formation should have begun at a very early age, but it is true. Nor will it help to blame ourselves—we are all amateur parents. What is important is what we can do now for our teens and for our younger children.

No matter how we responded to our children when they were younger, they need our verbal and nonverbal expressions of love and acceptance today. They need to be touched; *they need to be listened to.* Our listening conveys the message that they are valued, that they have something worthwhile to say. It also means you are not judging what is being said nor how it is being said. It means you can feed back to your teen what you have heard him say and how he is feeling. Does that sound like a big task? Perhaps it is, but it is necessary in *all* types of relationships.

Consider these questions about your own teen:

- How does he feel about himself?
- When does she feel good about herself?
- When does he feel down on himself?
- What are her values?
- What is important to him?
- What does she do to value herself?
- Has he learned self-assertion skills to handle peer pressure?

Have you asked your teen these questions? Have you asked in a way that will draw out answers? Discussing those answers with your teen will help him develop a more positive self-concept.

In addition to the above, you can *help him identify and accept his strengths and weaknesses.* How do you do that? Here's one way.

Suggest that your teen *and you* each list your own strengths and weaknesses, and then share them. Show him how you feel about the items on your list and what you might do to strengthen your weaknesses. Then see if your teen is willing to share his list. Be sure to listen, listen, listen! Do not judge him, and do not attempt to fix problems for him. Questions like, "What have you thought about trying?" may draw out some of his own problem-solving ability and help him use it.

Are you thinking, *Why should I write and share my own list?* Well, why not? Your teen needs your openness, vulnerability and modeling in order for him to grow and develop. Besides, you may be amazed at what you learn about yourself!

Encourage your teen. In 1 Thessalonians 5:11 we read: "Encourage . . . and build up one another." Be-

lieve in your teen. Help him set reasonable goals and plans, and then stand by him and let him know you are praying for him. Praise your teen and encourage him to develop a sense of pride in his accomplishments. Enjoy what he has both done and experienced, but help him to understand he does not have to become adequate through performance to gain importance in the sight of God. Rather, he has been given authentic value through what God has done for him in the gift of His Son.

Help your teen learn to:

- enjoy his own company
- listen to his own thoughts and feelings; and
- value who he is.

Reinforce him as a person so he can respect who he is and who he thinks he is. This is an excellent preventive when teens face peer pressure to conform.

Here are some positive beliefs you can share with your teen. You may want to ask him to evaluate each of these beliefs on a scale of 1 to 10 to see how strong or weak each belief is at this time.

EVALUATE YOUR BELIEFS

Positive, Healthy and Balanced Beliefs

- It is NOT necessary to be liked by everyone.
- I do NOT have to earn anyone's approval or acceptance to be a person of worth.
- I am a child of God. I'm deeply loved by Him, and I have been forgiven by Him; therefore, I am acceptable. I accept myself.
- My needs and wants are as important as other people's.

- Rejection is NOT terrible. It may be a bit unpleasant, but it is not terrible.

- Not being approved of or accepted by other people is NOT terrible. It may not be desirable, but it is not terrible.

- If somebody doesn't like me, I can live with it. I don't have to work feverishly to get him or her to like me.

- I can conquer my bad feelings by distinguishing the truth from misbelief.

- It is a misbelief that I must please other people and be approved by them.

- Jesus died on a cross for me so I can be free from the misbelief that other people decide my value.

A strong belief in these principles is vital, and repeating them to himself will be the best input a teen can get. It will do a great deal toward helping him develop a positive self-concept and thus be able to cope effectively with the stresses in his life.

The Word of God

Another way to help your teen is by showing him how to apply the Scriptures to life's upsets. Memorizing the Word of God and understanding both the meaning of the Scripture and how to apply it gives stability. One very helpful passage is James 1:2,3:

> Consider it all joy, my brethren, when you encounter various trials, knowing that the testing [or trying] of your faith produces endurance.

The word *consider,* or count, actually means an internal attitude of the heart or mind that determines

whether the trials and circumstances of life will affect us adversely or beneficially. Another way James 1:2 can be translated is: "Make up your mind to regard adversity as something to welcome or be glad about."

Each of us has the ability to decide what our attitude will be. We can approach a frustrating situation or a tragedy and say, "That's terrible. It's totally upsetting. That is the last thing I wanted to have happen. Why me, and why now?"

Or we can say, "It's not what I wanted, but it's here. I am disappointed and wish it hadn't turned out this way, but it did, so how can I make the best of it?"

It doesn't mean we won't experience pain, or disappointment, or an initial sense of frustration. We cannot deny that, but we can ask, "What can I learn from this? How can I respond to it so it doesn't control me or keep me from moving ahead with my life?"

There may be moments when a teen's responses to things that have happened seem totally negative. At these times we may have to remind him that he can choose to say, "I think there is a better way of responding to this. I want to see this from another perspective." God created all of us with the capacity to learn to respond this way. Ultimately, a person's view of God and of theology will affect how he or she handles a stress-producing crisis or situation.

We cannot insulate and protect our teens against the difficult times and stresses of life—and it is good that we can't. We would be doing them a disservice. Life IS difficult! Life is full of pressures and trials, but there is something we can do. We can assist our teens to learn—at an earlier age than many of us learned—how to face and handle stress through the resources provided by God. The opportunity to develop these skills

at an earlier age will give our teens greater stability.

When a teen experiences stress, it can have one of two influences on his relationship with God the same as when an adult is under stress. It can draw the teen closer, or it can cause him to turn away in bitterness and frustration. Isaiah 43:2 is an understanding and realistic description of stress, and it contains a promise:

> When you pass through the waters, I will be with you; and through the rivers, they will not overflow you. When you walk through the fire, you will not be scorched, nor will the flame burn you.

None of us is promised a life free of difficult situations, but we do have the promise that we are not alone when those things arise.

Our stability—and our teen's stability—comes from Christ Himself. He is our strength when we endeavor to help a teen in stress and crisis, and He is that teen's strength as well.

> Now to Him *who is able to establish you* according to my gospel and the preaching of Jesus Christ, according to the revelation of the mystery which has been kept secret for long ages past . . . (Romans 16:25, italics mine).

> Then he said to them, "Go, eat of the fat, drink of the sweet, and send portions to him who has nothing prepared; for this day is holy to our Lord. Do not be grieved, for the *joy of the LORD is your strength*" (Nehemiah 8:10, italics mine).

> And He shall be the *stability of your times,* a wealth of salvation, wisdom, and knowledge; the fear of the LORD is his treasure (Isaiah 33:6, italics mine).

APPENDIX

TEEN STRESS PROFILE

One of the best ways to help a teen cope with stress is to help him (or her) determine the degree of stress in his life. Below is a "Teen Scene Stress Test" you can give your teen.

One suggestion: Never use the word *test* to your teen, especially if you plan this on a weekend. *Inventory* or *profile* is a good substitute.

Before you suggest he do this, take a separate piece of paper and, relating the questions to your teen, answer them yourself from your own perspective as you have watched him handle stress. After he has completed the profile, let him know that you did it, too, from your observations of his handling stress and, if he's interested, you would be glad to share the results with him.

This quiz will enable you and your teenager to determine both the level of stress in his life right now and how well he handles it.

Your youngster should keep his answers just as honest and accurate as possible. If he is afraid to complete the profile or belligerently refuses to do so, encourage him in terms that he can understand and appreciate. Your teen needs you to point out that doing this inventory will put him more in touch with his own feelings and will help him understand why sometimes

he seems "out of it."

When your teen has finished, score the results and go through an explanation of the score with him. Then let him go back to his records and tapes while you review the test once more yourself. Did you predict your child's answers accurately? Do you know him as well as you thought? Don't be surprised if your answer to both of these questions is no. This profile is designed to help you better understand your child, the stress he is going through, and how you can help lessen it.

TEEN SCENE STRESS TEST

	OFTEN	SOMETIMES	SELDOM	NEVER
1. During the past three months, have you been under considerable strain, stress, or pressure?	—	—	—	—
2. Have you experienced any of the following symptoms: palpitations or a racing heart, dizziness, blushing, painfully cold hands or feet, shallow or fast breathing, nail biting, restless body or legs, butterflies in stomach, insomnia, chronic fatigue?	—	—	—	—
3. In general, do you have headaches or digestive upsets?	—	—	—	—

r

4. Do you have crying spells or feel like crying?   __ __ __ __

5. Do you have recurring nightmares?   __ __ __ __

6. Do you have pain in your neck, back, or arms?   __ __ __ __

7. Do you feel depressed or unhappy?   __ __ __ __

8. Do you worry excessively?   __ __ __ __

9. Do you ever feel anxious even though you don't know why?   __ __ __ __

10. Are you ever edgy or impatient with your parents or other family members?   __ __ __ __

11. Are you ever overwhelmed by hopelessness?   __ __ __ __

12. Do you dwell on things you should have done but didn't?   __ __ __ __

13. Do you dwell on things you did but shouldn't have?   __ __ __ __

14. Do you have any problems focusing on your schoolwork?   __ __ __ __

15. When you're criticized, do you brood about it?   __ __ __ __

16. Do you worry about what others think?   __ __ __ __

17. Are you bored?   __ __ __ __

18. Do you feel envy or resentment when someone has something you don't have?   __ __ __ __

19. Do you quarrel with your boyfriend/girlfriend?   __ __ __ __

20. Are there serious conflicts between your parents?   __ __ __ __

YES NO

21. Lately, do you find yourself more irritable and argumentative than usual? __ __

22. Are you as popular with friends as you'd wish? __ __

23. Are you doing as well in school as you'd like? __ __

24. Do you feel you can live up to your parents' expectations? __ __

25. Do you feel that your parents understand your problems and are supportive? __ __

26. On the whole, are you satisfied with the way you look? __ __

27. Do you have trouble with your teachers? __ __

28. Do you sometimes worry that your friends might be turning against you? __ __

29. Do you have enough spending money to cover your needs? __ __

30. Have you noticed lately that you eat, drink or smoke more than you really should? __ __

31. Do you make strong demands on yourself? __ __

32. Do you feel the limits imposed by your parents regarding what you may or may not do are justified? __ __

33. Do your parents always criticize you? __ __

34. Do you have any serious worries concerning your love relationships with the opposite sex? __ __

35. Are any of your brothers or sisters overly competitive with you? __ __

36. Do you feel left out of social gatherings? __ __

37. Do you habitually fall behind in your schoolwork? __ __

38. Do you feel tense and defensive when you're around someone your age of the

opposite sex? ___ ___

39. Have you, or has anyone in your family, suffered a severe illness or injury in the last year? ___ ___

40. Do you experience any conflict between your own standards and peer pressure to engage in certain activities? ___ ___

41. Have you recently moved to a new home, school or community? ___ ___

42. Have you been rejected by a boyfriend/girlfriend within the last three months? ___ ___

43. Is it very difficult for you to say no to requests? ___ ___

44. Have your grades taken a sudden drop lately? ___ ___

45. Do you often become ill after an emotional upset? ___ ___

Scoring: Add up your points based on this answer key:

	(a)	(b)	(c)	(d)		(a)	(b)	(c)	(d)
1.	7	4	1	0	11.	7	3	1	0
2.	7	4	1	0	12.	4	2	0	0
3.	6	3	1	0	13.	4	2	0	0
4.	5	2	1	0	14.	4	2	0	0
5.	6	3	1	0	15.	4	2	0	0
6.	4	2	0	0	16.	4	2	0	0
7.	7	3	1	0	17.	4	2	0	0
8.	6	3	1	0	18.	4	2	0	0
9.	6	3	1	0	19.	5	3	1	0
10.	5	2	0	0	20.	5	3	1	0

	Yes	No		Yes	No		Yes	No
21.	4	0	30.	5	0	38.	3	0
22.	0	3	31.	4	0	39.	6	0
23.	0	4	32.	0	3	40.	5	0
24.	0	5	33.	4	0	41.	3	0
25.	0	5	34.	5	0	42.	4	0
26.	0	4	35.	3	0	43.	3	0
27.	3	0	36.	4	0	44.	4	0
28.	4	0	37.	3	0	45.	5	0
29.	0	3						

WHAT YOUR SCORE MEANS

116-203. A score in this range indicates that your troubles outnumber your satisfactions and that you are currently subjected to a high level of stress. No doubt, you are already aware of your problems and are rightfully concerned.

You should do everything possible to avoid as many tense situations as you can until you feel more in control of your life. Review the quiz to pinpoint the major sources of your stress. Try to develop more effective ways of dealing with difficult human relationships and circumstances. Perhaps you are overreacting to problems or are not as willing to cope as you could be. Think about getting some kind of professional help. Sometimes even a few hours of counseling can be beneficial.

62-115. A score spanning this range signifies that the level of stress in your life is moderate, or that you are handling your frustrations quite well. However, because you have occasional difficulty managing the effects of stress, consider some new methods of overcoming disappointments. Remember, we all have to face and live with frustrations and anxieties.

0-61. A score in this range points to a relatively low stress level. In spite of minor worries and concerns, you are not in any serious trouble. You have good adaptive powers and are able to deal successfully with situations that make you temporarily uptight.[1]

NOTES

Chapter 1

1. Bettie B. Youngs, *Helping Your Teenager Deal With Stress* (Los Angeles, CA: Jeremy P. Tarcher, 1986), p. 66. Adapted.

Chapter 2

1. Donald C. Meadows, Barbara J. Porter and I. David Welch, *Children Under Stress* (Englewood Cliffs, NJ: Prentice-Hall, 1983), pp. 10-12.

2. Dr. Bettie B. Youngs, *Stress in Children* (New York: Avon Books, 1985), pp. 55-57. Adapted.

3. The survey, done by *Children and Teens Today* magazine, appeared in *Marriage and Divorce* 11:51 (July 21, 1986), n.p., from which we have quoted.

4. Mary Susan Miller, *Childstress* (Garden City, NY: Doubleday & Co., Inc., 1982), pp. 22-23.

5. Miller, *Childstress,* pp. 26-33. Adapted.

6. Meadows, *Children,* pp. 11-12.

Chapter 3

1. H. Norman Wright, *How to Have a Creative Crisis* (Waco, TX: Word Books, 1987).

2. David Eskind, *All Grown Up and No Place to Go* (Menlo Park, CA: Addison Wesley, 1982), pp. 168-77. Adapted.

3. Keith W. Sehnert, *Stress/Unstress* (Minneapolis: Augsburg, 1981), pp. 74-75. Adapted.

Chapter 4

1. G. Keith Olson, *Counseling Teenagers* (Loveland, CO: Group Books, 1984), pp. 36-37.

2. Antionette Saunders and Bonnie Remsberg, *The Stress-Proof Child* (New York: New American Library, 1984), pp. 31-32. Adapted.

3. Bettie B. Youngs, *Helping Your Teenager Deal With Stress* (Los Angeles: Jeremy P. Tarcher, 1986), pp. 95-97. Adapted.

Chapter 5

1. Jonathan Kellerman, *Helping the Fearful Child* (New York: W. W. Norton & Co., Inc., 1986).

Chapter 6

1. Brent Q. Hofen and Brenda Peterson, *The Crisis Intervention Handbook* (Englewood Cliffs, NJ: Prentice-Hall, 1982), pp. 21-39. Adapted.

2. E. Lindemann, "Symptometology and Management of Acute Grief," *American Journal of Psychiatry* (1981), 139:141-48.

3. G. Keith Olson, *Counseling Teenagers* (Loveland, CO: Group Books, 1984), pp. 27-28.

4. Frederick F. Flach and Suzanne C. Draughi, *The Nature and Treatment of Depression* (New York: Wiley, 1975), pp. 104-6. Adapted.

5. Bettie B. Youngs, *Helping Your Teenager Deal With Stress* (Los Anageles: Jeremy P. Tarcher, Inc., 1986), pp. 180-81. Adapted.

Chapter 7

1. Archibald Hart, *Children and Divorce: What to Expect and How to Help* (Waco, TX: Word Publishers, 1982), pp. 124-25.

2. *Marriage and Divorce Today* (May 18, 1987), 12:42, n.p.

3. H. Norman Wright, *Always Daddy's Girl* (Ventura, CA: Regal Books, n.d.).

4. H. Norman Wright, *Crisis Counseling* (San Bernardino, CA: Here's Life Publishers, 1986), pp. 167-172. Adapted.

Chapter 8

1. Tim Hansel, *When I Relax I Feel Guilty* (Elgin, IL: David C. Cook, 1979).

2. Dave and Jan Congo, *Less Stress* (Ventura, CA: Regal, n.d.).

3. H. Norman Wright, *How to Have a Creative Crisis* (Waco, TX: Word Books, 1987).

4. Mary Susan Miller, *Childstress* (Garden City, NY: Doubleday & Co., Inc., 1982), pp. 42-53. Adapted.

Chapter 9

1. H. Norman Wright, *How to Have a Creative Crisis* (Waco, TX: Word Books, 1987).

2. Charles R. Swindoll, *Growing Strong in the Seasons of Life* (Portland, OR: Multnomah Press, 1983), pp. 274-75.

3. David Eskind, *All Grown Up and No Place to Go* (Menlo Park, CA: Addison Wesley, 1982), pp. 200-214. Adapted.

4. Eskind, *All Grown Up*, pp. 200-214. Adapted.

Appendix

1. Bettie B. Youngs, *Helping Your Teenager Deal With Stress* (Los Angeles: Jeremy P. Tarcher, 1986), pp. 13-17.

Helping Your Kids Through Adolescence

Quantity   Total

____ **MOM AND DAD DON'T LIVE TOGETHER ANYMORE** *by Gary & Angela Hunt.* Help and encouragement for youth and their parents who are working through the confusing time of separation or divorce. ISBN 0-89840-199-2/$5.95 $____

____ **NOW THAT HE'S ASKED YOU OUT** *by Gary & Angela Hunt.* Straight talk for junior high girls . . . Focuses on key dating issues including: when she is old enough to date, what mature, Christian young men look for in a date and what role parents can play. ISBN 0-89840-258-1/$6.95 $____

____ **NOW THAT YOU'VE ASKED HER OUT** *by Gary & Angela Hunt.* Straight talk for junior high guys . . . Answers questions about when he is ready to date, curfews and dating guidelines, and relates facts about AIDS, teen pregnancy and abortion. ISBN 0-89840-259-X/$6.95 $____

____ **WHY TEENS ARE KILLING THEMSELVES: AND WHAT WE CAN DO ABOUT IT** *by Marion Duckworth.* This book explains why teens turn to suicide and what the home, church and community can do to prevent it. ISBN 0-89840-169-0/$8.95 $____

____ **SURVIVING THE TWEENAGE YEARS** *by Gary & Angela Hunt.* Walks parents and youth workers through the contradictory maze of preteen and early teen reactions to emotional, physical and mental changes in their lives. ISBN 0-89840-205-0/$6.95 $____

Indicate product(s) desired above. Fill out below.
Send to:

HERE'S LIFE PUBLISHERS, INC.
P. O. Box 1576
San Bernardino, CA 92402-1576

NAME_____

ADDRESS_____

STATE_____ZIP_____

☐ Payment (check or money order only) included

☐ Visa   ☐ Mastercard #_____

Expiration Date_____Signature_____

ORDER TOTAL	$_____
SHIPPING and HANDLING ($1.50 for one book, $0.50 for each additional. Do not exceed $4.00.)	$_____
APPLICABLE SALES TAX (CA, 6%)	$_____
TOTAL DUE	$_____

PAYABLE IN U.S. FUNDS.
(No cash orders accepted.)

**FOR FASTER SERVICE
CALL TOLL FREE:
1-800-950-4457**   Also ordering other side ☐   HKH 271-9

Your Christian bookstore should have these in stock. If not, use this "Shop-by-Mail" form.
PLEASE ALLOW 2 TO 4 WEEKS FOR DELIVERY.
PRICES SUBJECT TO CHANGE WITHOUT NOTICE.

BUILDING BETTER FAMILIES

Practical Resources
to Strengthen Your Home

Quantity   Total

____   **PULLING WEEDS, PLANTING SEEDS: Grow-** $_____
ing Character in Your Life and Family *by Den-*
nis Rainey. An inspiring collection of pointed
reflections on personal and family life with an abundance of practical insights for everyday living.
ISBN 0-89840-217-4/hardcover, $12.95

____   **THE DAD DIFFERENCE: Creating an En-** $_____
vironment for Your Child's Sexual Wholeness
by Josh McDowell and Dr. Norm Wakefield. Sets
the stage for fathering that will dramatically improve parent/teen relationships and reduce teen
sexual excesses. Practical examples of role modeling
and father/children activities.
ISBN 0-89840-252-2/$8.95

____   **PARENTING SOLO** *by Dr. Emil Authelet.* Take $_____
the fear—and some of the frustration—out of single
parenting. Helpful ideas for laying a strong biblical
foundation, understanding your need for healing,
and overcoming barriers that keep you and your
children from growing and enjoying a fulfilling life.
ISBN 0-89840-197-6/$7.95

Indicate product(s) desired above. Fill out below.
Send to:

HERE'S LIFE PUBLISHERS, INC.
P. O. Box 1576
San Bernardino, CA 92402-1576

NAME_____

ADDRESS_____

STATE_____ZIP_____

ORDER TOTAL $_____

SHIPPING and
HANDLING $_____
($1.50 for one book,
$0.50 for each additional.
Do not exceed $4.00.)

APPLICABLE
SALES TAX (CA, 6%)$_____

TOTAL DUE $_____

PAYABLE IN U.S. FUNDS.
(No cash orders accepted.)

☐ Payment (check or money order only)
   included
☐ Visa   ☐ Mastercard #_____

Expiration Date_____Signature_____

FOR FASTER SERVICE
CALL TOLL FREE:
1-800-950-4457   Also ordering other side ☐   HKH 271-9